modern
italian
cooking

hamlyn

This edition first published in the U.K. in 1999
by Hamlyn, a division of Octopus Publishing Group Limited
2–4 Heron Quays, London E14 4JP

Reprinted 2001

Copyright © 1999, 2001 Octopus Publishing Group Ltd

ISBN 0 600 60544 2

Printed in Hong Kong

NOTES
Both metric and imperial measurements have been given in all recipes. Use one set of measurements only, and not a mixture of both.

Standard level spoon measurements are used in all recipes.
1 tablespoon = one 15 ml spoon
1 teaspoon = one 5 ml spoon

Eggs should be medium to large unless otherwise stated. The Department of Health advises that eggs should not be consumed raw. This book contains dishes made with raw or lightly cooked eggs. It is prudent for more vulnerable people such as pregnant and nursing mothers, invalids, the elderly, babies and young children to avoid uncooked or lightly cooked dishes made with eggs. Once prepared, these dishes should be kept refrigerated and used promptly.

Meat and poultry should be cooked thoroughly. To test if poultry is cooked, pierce the flesh through the thickest part with a skewer or fork — the juices should run clear, never pink or red. Do not re-freeze poultry that has been frozen previously and thawed. Do not re-freeze a cooked dish that has been frozen previously.

Milk should be full fat unless otherwise stated.

Nut and Nut Derivatives
This book includes dishes made with nuts and nut derivatives. It is advisable for customers with known allergic reactions to nuts and nut derivatives and those who may be potentially vulnerable to these allergies, such as pregnant and nursing mothers, invalids, the elderly, babies and children to avoid dishes made with nuts and nut oils. It is also prudent to check the labels of pre-prepared ingredients for the possible inclusion of nut derivatives.

Pepper should be freshly ground black pepper unless otherwise stated.

Fresh herbs should be used, unless otherwise stated. If unavailable, use dried herbs as an alternative, but halve the quantities stated.

Measurements for canned food have been given as a standard metric equivalent.

Ovens should be pre-heated to the specified temperature — if using a fan-assisted oven, follow the manufacturer's instructions for adjusting the time and the temperature.

Vegetarians should look for the 'V' symbol on a cheese to ensure it is made with vegetarian rennet. There are vegetarian forms of Parmesan, feta, Cheddar, Cheshire, Red Leicester, dolcelatte and many goats' cheeses, among others.

Contents

Introduction

Think of Italian food and you will immediately be transported to the warm, scented air of the Mediterranean, or to a Sicilian orange grove, or to the earthy sweetness of a wooded vine- and olive-clad Tuscan hill. Either way, the thought will conjure up warm, happy visions of a life in sunnier climes. You will be reminded of places that you have enjoyed visiting on holiday, evoking joyful memories of carefree eating and drinking. This type of cooking is sunny, warm-hearted and generous – rather like the people. The ingredients are fresh, flavoursome and kissed by the sun.

In the main, Italy doesn't suffer, as we unfortunately do nowadays, from produce that has been picked when it was unripe, transported from the other side of the world in refrigerated containers, and sold to us in our shops with little of its true and original flavour. Most of the produce in Italy, especially in the markets, is homegrown and fresh, and it is always seasonal. As one thing goes out of season, something else takes its place. As a result, food becomes special, each season bringing with it its own long-awaited bounty.

There are seasons for fruit, vegetables, herbs, nuts, cheeses, types of bread, mushrooms, grapes and wine, and olives. The seasons in Italy are celebrated in *sagras*, or festivals, all over the country. There might be the *sagra* of the chestnut in Tuscany, for example, or the *sagra* of the salami in a little village in the north – all confirming the importance of the seasons and of fresh produce in the lives of the people.

'Think of Italian food and you will immediately be transported to the warm, scented air of the Mediterranean, ...'

To some extent, unfortunately, we have lost this way of life and this immediacy in Britain, but a visit to an Italian market while you are on holiday will soon open your eyes and serve as a salutary reminder. There is great joy in selecting the best seasonal produce rather than raiding the freezer for things that grew and were harvested many moons ago.

Food in Italy starts with the shopping. Traditional Italian cooks don't shop in the supermarket – they go to the market and select, examining, comparing and finally choosing, the best of whatever is on display: the shiniest peppers, the crispest lettuce, the greenest spinach, the biggest peaches, the plumpest chicken, the tiniest squid, the youngest and sweetest peas. They choose produce in the knowledge that each and every ingredient really matters, because all the ingredients contribute their own special, individual flavour, colour and texture to the finished dish.

The Italians really understand the enormous importance of food. They enjoy everything about it. They like thinking about it, talking about it, shopping for it, preparing it and eating it, and they do each of these things wholeheartedly. Food is a necessity – but it is also much more than that. It is a pleasure to be shared by everyone. It is life itself.

The recipes in this book encompass the essence of the diverse cooking in Italy. They are all based on authentic recipes – many of them traditional ones that have been cooked in Italy for generations. Cook them now and bring a touch of the real Italy into your own home.

Following are recipes for chicken, beef, vegetable and fish stock. You will find it very useful to refer to these basic recipes as they are required for many of the recipes throughout the book. If you are making fish stock, you should be able to find the bones you need at your local fishmonger.

Once made, the stocks can be cooled and then frozen. Freeze stock in small batches in plastic tubs or ice cube trays. When they have been frozen, the cubes can be transferred to clearly labelled plastic bags for ease of storage.

Every cook should be aware that a few basic rules are necessary in the making of a good stock. If you follow these, you will find that your finished dishes will taste a whole lot better.

Stock should always be simmered extremely gently, or it will evaporate too quickly and become cloudy. Never add salt to the stock as simmering will reduce it and concentrate the flavour. This will obviously affect the flavour of the finished dish. Any scum that rises to the surface should be removed as it appears, otherwise it will spoil both the colour and the flavour of the stock.

Chicken stock

Chicken stock is probably one of the most useful stocks that you can have in your freezer. It is suitable for use in a great many recipes – other, of course, than vegetarian ones.

1 cooked chicken carcass
raw chicken giblets
1 onion, roughly chopped
2 large carrots, roughly chopped
1 celery stick, roughly chopped
1 bay leaf
a few parsley stalks, lightly crushed
1 thyme sprig
1.8 litres/3 pints cold water

1 Chop the chicken carcass into 3 or 4 pieces and place in a large saucepan with the giblets and trimmings. Add the onion, carrots, celery, bay leaf, parsley stalks and thyme. Cover with the cold water.

2 Bring to the boil, removing any scum from the surface. Lower the heat and simmer for 2–2½ hours. Strain the stock through a muslin-lined sieve and leave to cool thoroughly before refrigerating.

Makes: **about 1 litre/1¾ pints**

Preparation time: 5–10 minutes

Cooking time: about 2½ hours

Beef stock

Beef stock is a rich addition to many meat recipes and adds a truly delicious flavour that it is impossible to create with commercial stock cubes or granules.

750 g/1½ lb boneless shin of beef, cubed
2 onions, chopped
2–3 carrots, chopped
2 celery sticks, chopped
1 bay leaf
1 bouquet garni (2 parsley sprigs, 2 thyme sprigs and 1 bay leaf)
4–6 black peppercorns
1.8 litres/3 pints water

1 Place the beef in a large saucepan with the onion, carrots, celery, bay leaf, bouquet garni and peppercorns.

2 Cover with the water and slowly bring to the boil. As soon as it comes to the boil, reduce the heat to a gentle simmer. Cover with a well-fitting lid and simmer for 4 hours, removing any scum from the surface.

3 Strain the stock through a muslin-lined sieve and leave to cool thoroughly before refrigerating.

Makes: **about 1.5 litres/2½ pints**

Preparation time: 15 minutes

Cooking time: about 4½ hours

Fresh stock

A good stock is easy, satisfying and cheap to make, and uses only a few basic ingredients. Commercial stock cubes and granules are a lot better than they used to be, but they simply don't compare with the real thing. It is a great shame to resort to stock cubes when the true flavour of a delicious homemade broth is far preferable and easy to achieve.

2 Cover with the water. Bring to the boil and simmer gently for 30 minutes, skimming off any scum when necessary. Strain and cool the stock completely before refrigerating.

Makes: **1 litre/1¾ pints**

Preparation time: 5–10 minutes

Cooking time: about 45 minutes

Fish stock

When purchasing the trimmings for this stock, oily fish should be avoided. It is also very important that the stock does not boil as it will become very cloudy.

1.5 kg/3 lb fish trimmings
1 onion, sliced
1 small leek, green part removed
1 celery stick
1 bay leaf
6 parsley stalks
10 peppercorns
475 ml/16 fl oz dry white wine
1.8 litres/3 pints water

1 Put the fish trimmings in a large pan with the onion, leek, celery, bay leaf, parsley stalks, peppercorns and wine.

2 Cover with the water and slowly bring to just below boiling point. Simmer for 20 minutes, removing any scum from the surface. Strain the stock through a muslin-lined sieve and leave to cool before refrigerating.

Makes: **1.8 litres/3 pints**

Preparation time: 10 minutes

Cooking time: 30 minutes

Vegetable stock

This recipe for vegetable stock can be varied to your own taste, and adapted according to what vegetables you have available. For example, you can try adding some fennel for a mild aniseed flavour or a sliver of orange zest for an added lift. The addition of tomatoes will give the stock extra richness of flavour and colour. Remember to avoid using any floury root vegetables, such as potatoes, as they will cause the stock to become unattractively cloudy.

500 g/1 lb chopped mixed vegetables, such as equal quantities of carrots, leeks, celery, onion and mushrooms
1 garlic clove
6 peppercorns
1 bouquet garni (2 parsley sprigs, 2 thyme sprigs and 1 bay leaf)
1.2 litres/2 pints water

1 Place the chopped vegetables and garlic in a large saucepan and add the peppercorns and bouquet garni.

Basic pizza dough

A basic pizza dough is quick and easy to make, and will come in useful for preparing delicious homemade pizzas or a less refined focaccia.

25 g/1 oz fresh yeast, or 2 tablespoons dried
   active baking yeast, or 2 sachets easy-blend
   yeast
pinch of sugar
250 ml/8 fl oz warm water
375 g/12 oz Italian 00 flour, or 250 g/8 oz Italian
   00 flour sifted with 125 g/4 oz rye flour
2 tablespoons olive oil
1 teaspoon coarse sea salt or crystal salt

1 If you are using fresh yeast, cream it with the sugar in a medium bowl, then whisk in the warm water. Leave for 10 minutes until frothy. For other yeasts, refer to packet instructions.

2 Sift the flour into a large bowl and make a well in the centre. Pour in the yeast mixture, olive oil and salt, and mix together with a round-bladed knife, then with your hand, until the dough comes together.

3 Tip out the dough on to a floured surface. Wash and dry your hands, then knead the dough for about 10 minutes until it is smooth and elastic. It should be quite soft, but if it is too soft to handle, add a little more flour.

4 Place the dough in a clean, oiled bowl, cover with a damp tea towel and leave to rise until doubled in size. This should take about 1 hour.

Makes: **two 25–30 cm/10–12 inch thin crust pizza bases**

Preparation time: 25 minutes, plus rising

'...or to the earthy sweetness of a wooded vine- and olive-clad Tuscan hill.'

different perforations, so you can choose large or small holes to grate the cheese coarsely or finely. They can also be used to grate other foods, such as carrots, chocolate or citrus rind.

If you are going to make your own pasta, you will also need a rolling pin for rolling out the pasta dough. Rolling pins are usually made from wood or marble. Choose a heavy rolling pin, as this makes rolling easier, and always flour both the work surface and the rolling pin lightly every time you make pasta. Always wipe a rolling pin before putting it away.

A ravioli cutter is useful for making ravioli. It consists of a fluted-edged metal cutter with a wooden handle, and is used to stamp out individual ravioli or other flat pasta shapes. Ravioli cutters are made in a variety of different sizes and shapes, including circles and squares. A ravioli mould is a metal tray with a series of indentations for cutting out ravioli shapes in large numbers. A small rolling pin is sometimes provided with a ravioli mould.

A garlic press is another essential item, given that garlic is such a basic ingredient used in Italian cooking. A mezzaluna is also useful – a half moon-shaped blade, with one or two handles, for chopping mushrooms, fresh herbs and so on, using a simple rocking motion. Mezzalunas sometimes come with their own wooden chopping bowl.

If you intend to make pizzas, a pizza brick is a useful tool. This is usually made of terracotta and is used to bake pizzas and flat breads instead of a baking sheet. It retains the heat well and crisps the bottom of the pizza during the baking process. Traditional pizzas are always baked on a pizza brick. The brick should have a raised foot to allow an easy grip when removing it from the oven.

A pizza wheel is also useful. This is a multi-purpose implement for cutting out pizza slices, pastry and pasta. When you choose a cutter, make sure that the wheel turns freely.

Italian cooking utensils

There are not many special tools that are required for Italian cooking, but there are a few that will make the job easier. Always buy tools that are dishwasher-safe, if necessary, including a range of saucepans, sharp knives and whisks. Buy the best that you can afford and look after them all carefully.

Assuming that you will be making a lot of pasta dishes, perhaps the number one necessity is a pasta server. This is an inexpensive tool, but absolutely essential. It is a long-handled spoon, made of stainless steel or plastic, which is used for transferring pasta from the saucepan to the serving dish or plates. This useful gadget has teeth which grip long strands of spaghetti or tagliatelle firmly but gently, while the water drains away through the hole in the middle.

Cheese graters are indispensable and come in a variety of forms – either as a flat sheet, a box shape, or a drum with a turning handle. Either way, they usually have a selection of

Classic Fresh Italian Flavours

Tomatoes

The Italian for tomato is *pomodoro*, which literally means 'golden apple'. Although tomatoes are a relative newcomer to Italian cuisine (from the discovery of the New World), they have become an essential ingredient in many Italian dishes, especially those from the south. Fresh ripe tomatoes should be slightly soft, bright red and sweet. Plum tomatoes are most commonly used for making sauces. When fresh tomatoes are not available, canned and bottled ones are an acceptable substitute.

Herbs

Fresh herbs are considerably better than dried ones, and parsley, sage, rosemary, mint, thyme, marjoram and oregano are all widely used in Italian cooking. Basil is perhaps the most widely used Italian herb of all. It has bright green leaves and a pungent, aromatic, slightly spicy flavour that goes particularly well with tomatoes. Used to flavour tomato sauces, stews and casseroles, it is the essential ingredient in pesto sauce and is also often used in salads. If you are adding it to a hot sauce, wait until the end of the cooking time, as it doesn't respond well to heat. It can be bought in many good supermarkets, either in packets or growing in pots. Basil doesn't keep well, so buy it as you need it and store wrapped in damp kitchen paper or in a plastic bag in the vegetable drawer of the refrigerator.

Rocket

Known in Italy as *arugola*, rocket has a distinctive peppery flavour and is often added to salads. It is, in fact, part of the cabbage family. It is available in many supermarkets, and can also be grown at home. Store it in a plastic bag in the vegetable drawer of the refrigerator.

Spinach

Spinach is a favourite Italian ingredient. The small, young, vibrantly coloured leaves are perfect for eating raw in salads. Its distinctive flavour goes particularly well with cheese, meat and fish dishes. It is also used in Italian cooking for adding both flavour and colour to fresh and dried pasta and gnocchi.

Radicchio

Part of the chicory family, radicchio has deep red leaves patterned with white, and a distinctively bitter flavour. It is usually served as part of a mixed salad, where it both looks and tastes marvellous. Store it in a plastic bag in the vegetable drawer of the refrigerator.

Garlic

Garlic is an integral part of just about every Italian recipe, including sauces, salads, pizzas and stews. Select your garlic bulbs carefully, remembering that the larger the cloves, the sweeter the garlic will be. Small garlic cloves tend to be bitter and strong. The softer and fresher the garlic, the more subtle the flavour.

Breads

There are many specialist Italian breads, which are available in Italian delicatessens and in some good supermarkets. Try ciabatta, for example, which is one of the most popular Italian breads, baked with a slightly open texture and sometimes flavoured with sun-dried tomatoes or olives. Another delicious Italian bread is focaccia, which is a flat yeast bread made with olive oil and served with different toppings such as sun-dried tomatoes, olives or herbs.

Panettone

This is a yeast cake, made with candied fruit. It is a speciality of northern Italy and is often served on special occasions, such as Christmas and Easter.

Cured hams

There are several cured raw hams that are eaten in Italy, the most famous ones being Parma and San Daniele, both of which command a high price and have a salty yet slightly sweet taste. They are sliced wafer-thin and are often served as an antipasto dish with melon or fresh figs.

Mortadella

Mortadella is a large, slightly smoked sausage, which is made from pure pork, finely minced, or from a mixture of different meats. It is seasoned with parsley and studded with olives and pistachio nuts. It is finely sliced and eaten cold as part of a salad or in sandwiches.

Salami

There are countless varieties of regional salami in Italy. It is often served sliced as an antipasto and is also good in sandwiches and as an addition to salads.

Parmesan

This is Italy's most famous cheese, which comes from Parma, and should never be missing from your refrigerator. *Parmigiano Reggiano* is the best. It is expensive, but a little goes a long way and it is worth every penny. It is a very hard cheese made from cows' milk and is aged over a long period of time – for at least a year and sometimes for as long as three years. It is best to buy it in a block and grate it freshly yourself over pasta dishes as you need it – the flavour diminishes rapidly once it has been grated, and the ready-grated type that you can buy in a vacuum pack from the supermarket is very inferior. You can also shave it attractively over dishes using a vegetable peeler. It keeps well in the refrigerator wrapped in foil or in a plastic bag, and it also freezes well.

Pecorino Romano

This is a hard cheese for grating rather like Parmesan, and is used in much the same way. It is made from sheep's milk, which gives it a distinctive salty flavour. The name comes from the word *pecora*, which means 'ewe'.

Mozzarella

Mozzarella is a fresh white curd cheese which is traditionally made from buffalo milk. It is now often made from cows' milk, though this is, quite simply, not in the same league. It is sold packaged in its own whey, which keeps it moist. It has a soft, chewy, almost rubbery texture – though not an unpleasant one – and a bland, milky flavour. It melts to a delicious stringiness when heated, and is a classic topping for pizza. It is an important ingredient in Italian cooking, along with tomatoes and basil. As a general rule, use cows' milk mozzarella for cooking, and the more expensive buffalo mozzarella raw.

Soups

White Bean Soup with Toasted Garlic and Chilli Oil

This is a substantial white bean peasant soup from Tuscany. To give it a sophisticated touch, sliced garlic is fried until golden in chilli-flavoured olive oil, then poured over the soup at the last moment. This soup is often served as a main course, ladled over toasted country bread.

Serves: **6**

Preparation time: 35 minutes

Cooking time: 1 hour 10 minutes

Oven temperature: 160°C/325°F/Gas Mark 3

250 g/8 oz dried white beans (haricot, cannellini, etc.), soaked overnight in cold water
Chicken or Vegetable Stock (see pages 8 and 9) or cold water
handful of sage leaves
4 garlic cloves
150 ml/¼ pint olive oil
2 tablespoons chopped sage or rosemary
good pinch of chilli flakes
salt and pepper
roughly chopped parsley, to garnish

1 Drain the beans and place them in a flameproof casserole. Cover with cold water or chicken or vegetable stock to a height of 5 cm/2 inches above the beans, and push in the sage leaves. Bring the beans to the boil, then cover them tightly and bake in a preheated oven, 160°C/325°F/Gas Mark 3, for about 1 hour or until tender. The beans may not take this long, depending on their freshness, so test them after 40 minutes. Leave them in their cooking liquid.

2 Meanwhile, finely chop half of the garlic, and thinly slice the remainder.

3 Put half of the beans, the cooked sage and all the liquid into a food processor or blender and whizz until smooth. Pour the purée back into the casserole with the remaining beans. If the soup is thicker than liked, add extra water or stock to thin it.

4 Heat half of the olive oil in a frying pan and add the chopped garlic. Fry gently until it is soft and golden then add the herbs and cook for 30 seconds. Stir the mixture into the soup and reheat until boiling. Simmer gently for 10 minutes. Taste and season well with salt and pepper. Pour into a warmed tureen or ladle into warmed soup bowls.

5 Fry the sliced garlic carefully in the remaining olive oil until golden (don't let it go too dark or it will be bitter), then stir in the chilli flakes. Dip the base of the pan into cold water to stop the garlic cooking then spoon the garlic and oil over the soup. Serve sprinkled with chopped parsley.

Roasted Pepper Soup with Black Pepper Cream

The smoky sweet flavour of roasted peppers needs the pungency of black pepper to provide a kick. The use of black pepper is fundamental to much Italian cooking, especially in the north.

Serves: **4**

Preparation time: 20 minutes

Cooking time: 1 hour

Oven temperature: 240°C/475°F/Gas Mark 9

6 large red or yellow peppers
4 leeks, white and pale green parts only, thinly
   sliced
3 tablespoons olive oil
750 ml/1¼ pints Chicken or Vegetable Stock
   (see pages 8 and 9)
2 teaspoons black peppercorns
75 ml/3 fl oz mascarpone cheese
75 ml/3 fl oz milk
salt and pepper
toasted country bread, to serve

FOOD FACT • Mascarpone is a soft cream cheese, so rich that it is more like cream than cheese. It is available in this country in most big supermarkets, packed in small plastic tubs.

1 Place the peppers in a large roasting tin and roast in a preheated oven, 240°C/475°F/Gas Mark 9, for 20–30 minutes, turning once, until they begin to char. Remove the peppers from the oven, put them into a polythene bag and close it tightly. Leave for 10 minutes to steam.

2 Put the leeks into a bowl of cold water to soak for 5 minutes.

3 Remove the peppers from the bag and peel off the skins, then pull out the stalks – the seeds should come with them. Halve the peppers, scrape out any remaining seeds and roughly chop the flesh. Swish the leeks around in the water to loosen any mud, then drain and rinse well.

4 Heat the oil in a large saucepan, add the leeks and cook gently for 10 minutes until soft but not coloured. Add the peppers, stock and a little salt and pepper. Bring the mixture to the boil then turn down the heat and simmer for 20 minutes.

5 Pound or grind the black peppercorns as finely as possible. Beat the mascarpone with the milk and pepper. Season with salt and chill until needed.

6 Liquidize the soup in a blender, then pass it through a sieve back into the rinsed out pan. Reheat, taste and adjust the seasoning if necessary. Serve the soup in warmed bowls with dollops of the pepper cream and slices of toasted country bread.

Pumpkin and Garlic Soup

Roasting the pumpkin and garlic together concentrates the flavour of the pumpkin, which can be bland.

Serves: **6–8**

Preparation time: 30 minutes

Cooking time: 50 minutes

Oven temperature: 200°C/400°F/Gas Mark 6

FOOD FACT • Look for a variety of pumpkin with bright orange flesh, or try using butternut squash instead.

750 g/1½ lb pumpkin
6 garlic cloves, unpeeled
4 tablespoons olive oil
2 onions, finely sliced
2 celery sticks, chopped
50 g/2 oz long-grain white rice
1.5 litres/2½ pints Chicken or Vegetable Stock
 (see pages 8 and 9) or water
salt and pepper
4 tablespoons chopped parsley, to serve
PARMESAN CRISPS
125 g/4 oz freshly grated Parmesan
a few fennel seeds (optional)
fresh red chilli, finely chopped (optional)

1 Scrape out the seeds from the pumpkin, cut off the skin and cut the flesh into large cubes. Place them in a roasting tin with the garlic cloves and toss with 2 tablespoons of the olive oil. Do not crowd the tin – use 2 tins if necessary. Roast in a preheated oven, 200°C/400°F/Gas Mark 6, for about 30 minutes until the pumpkin is very tender and beginning to brown a little.

2 Heat the remaining olive oil in a large saucepan and add the onions and celery. Cook over a gentle heat for 10 minutes until they are just beginning to brown and soften. Stir in the rice and pour in the stock or water. Bring to the boil, cover the pan and simmer for about 15–20 minutes until the rice is tender.

3 Remove the pumpkin and garlic from the oven and let them cool slightly. Then pop the garlic cloves out of their skins. Add the garlic and pumpkin to the saucepan, bring to the boil and simmer for 10 minutes.

4 Meanwhile, to make the Parmesan crisps, first line a baking sheet with non-stick baking parchment. Spoon small mounds of cheese onto the paper at regular intervals. Flatten with the back of a spoon. Sprinkle some fennel seeds and chopped chilli on top, if liked.

5 Bake the crisps in a preheated oven, 200°C/400°F/Gas Mark 6, for 3–6 minutes until golden. Remove from the oven and leave for a couple of minutes to set, or, if you prefer, curl them over a rolling pin or a wooden spoon at this stage. Carefully lift them off the paper. Put to one side and leave to cool completely.

6 Liquidize or roughly blend the soup and return it to the pan. Taste and season with salt and plenty of freshly ground black pepper. Add extra stock or water if the soup is too thick.

7 To serve, reheat the soup and stir in the parsley. The Parmesan crisps can be either served separately in a bowl or sprinkled over the soup.

Chestnut Soup

Preparing the chestnuts for this soup is a bit of a chore, but the flavour is absolutely wonderful.

Serves: **6**

Preparation time: 20 minutes

Cooking time: 1 hour

750 g/1½ lb fresh, plump, sweet chestnuts or
   400 g/13 oz dried chestnuts, soaked overnight
   in cold water
125 g/4 oz butter
150 g/5 oz pancetta or streaky bacon, chopped
2 onions, finely chopped
1 carrot, chopped
1 celery stick, chopped
1 tablespoon chopped rosemary
2 bay leaves
2 garlic cloves, halved
salt and pepper
rosemary sprigs, to garnish

1 If you are using fresh chestnuts, the skins will have to be removed before cooking. To do this, use a small sharp knife to slit the shell of each chestnut across the rounded side. Put the chestnuts into a saucepan and cover them with cold water. Bring to the boil and simmer for 15–20 minutes. Remove the pan from the heat and lift out the chestnuts. Peel off the thick outer skin, then peel away the thinner inner skin, which has a bitter taste.

2 Melt the butter in a large saucepan and add the pancetta or bacon. Fry over a moderate heat until beginning to turn golden. Add the chopped onions, carrot and celery and cook for 5–10 minutes until they are beginning to soften and brown.

3 Add the chestnuts to the pan with the chopped rosemary, bay leaves, garlic and enough water to completely cover. Bring to the boil, half-cover the pan, turn down the heat and simmer for 30 minutes, stirring occasionally. The chestnuts should start to disintegrate and thicken the soup. Taste and season well. Garnish the soup with rosemary sprigs and serve in warmed bowls.

Fennel and Lemon Soup with Black Olive Gremolata

Fennel, lemon and ripe black olives are a perfect combination of flavours. To give this soup a summery flavour, use the fat salad onions, like giant spring onions, which you sometimes see in bunches in early summer. The olives must be the Greek-style crinkled black olives with their full ripe fruity flavour, and there mustn't be any white pith left on the lemon rind.

Serves: **4**

Preparation time: 20 minutes

Cooking time: 40 minutes

75 ml/3 fl oz extra virgin olive oil
3 fat salad onions, chopped
250 g/8 oz fennel, trimmed, cored and thinly sliced, reserving any green fronds for the gremolata and chopping them finely
1 potato, diced
finely grated rind and juice of 1 lemon
750 ml/1¼ pints Chicken or Vegetable Stock (see pages 8 and 9)
salt and pepper

BLACK OLIVE GREMOLATA
1 small garlic clove, finely chopped
finely grated rind of 1 lemon
4 tablespoons chopped parsley
16 Greek-style black olives, pitted and chopped

1 Heat the oil in a large saucepan, add the onions and cook for 5–10 minutes until beginning to soften. Add the fennel, potato and lemon rind, and cook for 5 minutes until the fennel begins to soften. Pour in the stock and bring to the boil. Turn down the heat, cover the pan and simmer for about 25 minutes or until the ingredients are tender.

2 To make the gremolata, mix together the garlic, lemon rind, chopped fennel fronds and parsley then stir the chopped olives into the herb mixture. Cover and chill.

3 Liquidize the soup and pass it through a sieve to remove any strings of fennel. The soup should not be too thick, so add more stock if necessary. Return it to the rinsed pan. Taste and season well with salt, pepper and plenty of lemon juice. Pour into warmed bowls and sprinkle each serving with a portion of the gremolata, to be stirred in before eating.

VARIATION • Use a bunch of spring onions instead of the 3 fat salad onions.

Tuscan Bean and Vegetable Soup

This is a great soup for a family get-together, best made in quantity and very filling. The Italian name of the soup, la ribollita, *literally means reboiled, as the basic bean and vegetable soup is made the day before then reheated. It is ladled over toasted garlic bread, drizzled with olive oil and served with lots of Parmesan cheese.*

Serves: **8 generously**

Preparation time: 30 minutes

Cooking time: about 3 hours

150 ml/¼ pint extra virgin olive oil
1 onion, finely chopped
1 carrot, chopped
1 celery stick, chopped
2 leeks, finely chopped
4 garlic cloves, finely chopped
1 small white cabbage, shredded
1 large potato, chopped
4 courgettes, chopped
200 g/7 oz dried cannellini beans, soaked
    overnight in cold water, rinsed and drained
400 g/13 oz passata (strained crushed tomatoes)
2 rosemary sprigs
2 thyme sprigs
2 sage sprigs
1 dried red chilli
about 2 litres/3½ pints water
500 g/1 lb cavolo nero (Tuscan black cabbage)
    or Savoy cabbage, finely shredded
6 thick slices of coarse crusty white bread
1 garlic clove, bruised
salt and pepper
TO SERVE
extra virgin olive oil
freshly grated Parmesan cheese

1 Heat half of the olive oil in a heavy saucepan and add the onion, carrot and celery. Cook gently for about 10 minutes, stirring frequently. Next add the leeks and finely chopped garlic and cook for another 10 minutes. Add the cabbage, potato and courgettes, stir well and cook for a further 10 minutes, stirring frequently.

2 Stir in the soaked beans, passata, rosemary, thyme and sage, dried chilli, salt and plenty of black pepper. Cover with the water (the vegetables should be well covered) and bring to the boil, then turn down the heat and simmer, covered, for at least 2 hours, until the beans are very soft.

3 Remove 2–3 ladlefuls of soup, mash it well then return to the soup. Stir in the cavolo nero or Savoy cabbage and simmer for another 15 minutes. Leave the soup to cool then refrigerate overnight.

4 The next day, slowly reheat the soup and stir in the remaining olive oil. Toast the bread and rub it with the bruised garlic. Arrange the bread over the base of a tureen or in individual bowls and ladle the soup over it. Drizzle with extra olive oil and serve with plenty of freshly grated Parmesan.

VARIATION • Strictly speaking, this soup should be made with the delicious Tuscan black cabbage, called cavolo nero, but you can use Savoy cabbage, too.

Sicilian Fish Soup

On Fridays and market days in coastal Sicily, tiny vans sell fresh fish on street corners. Piles of mixed small fish are especially set aside for fish soup, and there will also be squid, shellfish and large prawns. A well-flavoured broth is made with saffron and fennel seeds, and the fish, prawns, shellfish and squid are poached in it. The fish is served first and the broth is ladled on top.

Serves: **6–8**

Preparation time: 30 minutes

Cooking time: 45 minutes

1 kg/2 lb fresh mussels and clams, scrubbed and debearded
500 g/1 lb small squid, cleaned, tentacles removed and sliced into rings
500 g/1 lb raw medium or large prawns, peeled
1.75 kg/3½ lb whole mixed fish (see below), cleaned

BROTH

150 ml/¼ pint extra virgin olive oil
4 leeks, sliced
4 garlic cloves, finely chopped
300 ml/½ pint dry white wine
large pinch of saffron threads
750 g/1½ lb ripe red plum tomatoes, roughly chopped
2 tablespoons sun-dried tomato purée or 6 sun-dried tomatoes in oil, drained and roughly chopped
1 teaspoon fennel seeds
1 tablespoon dried oregano
600 ml/1 pint water
salt and pepper
chopped parsley, to garnish

1 First make the broth. Heat the olive oil in a large, deep, flameproof earthenware casserole, add the leeks and garlic and cook gently for about 5 minutes until the leeks are softening. Pour in the white wine and boil rapidly until reduced by half, then add the saffron, tomatoes, sun-dried tomato purée or sun-dried tomatoes, fennel seeds and dried oregano. Pour in the water and bring to the boil. Turn down the heat, cover the casserole and simmer for 20 minutes until the tomatoes and oil separate.

2 Place the mussels and clams in a bowl of cold water.

3 Cook the seafood as follows. Add the squid to the casserole and poach for 3–4 minutes. Remove with a slotted spoon, cover and keep warm. Add the prawns and simmer until opaque and cooked. Remove with a slotted spoon and keep warm with the squid. Drain the mussels and clams and add to the broth, cover and boil for a few minutes until they open. Remove with a slotted spoon and keep warm, discarding any that have not opened. Poach all the remaining fish until just cooked then remove them from the broth.

4 To serve, arrange all the fish on a serving dish with the mussels and clams, squid and prawns on top. Taste and season the broth. Moisten the fish with some of the broth and serve the rest of the broth separately. Garnish with chopped parsley.

FOOD FACT • Choose at least four varieties of fish to make this soup, excluding oily fish like salmon, herring or sardines – the greater the variety, the more intense the flavour of the soup. Besides shellfish, choose from conger eel, red gurnard, cod, hake, John Dory, red mullet, monkfish, shark, swordfish, weever, whiting and wrasse.

Clam and Courgette Soup

This light fresh soup of courgettes and clams is called aquacotta, which means, literally, cooked water. It is a simple soup, made more substantial by ladling it over toasted bread, as they do in the country.

Serves: **4**

Preparation time: 15 minutes

Cooking time: 25 minutes

750 g/1½ lb fresh baby clams or cockles, cleaned
3 tablespoons olive oil
2 large garlic cloves, 1 finely chopped and 1 bruised
750 g/1½ lb courgettes, thickly sliced
finely grated rind and juice of 1 lemon
1 tablespoon chopped marjoram
about 1 litre/1¾ pints Vegetable Stock (see page 9) or water
4 thick slices of country bread, toasted
salt and pepper
extra olive oil, to serve

1 Bring 1 cm/½ inch water to the boil in a saucepan, add the clams and steam until they open. Reserve the juice and remove half of the clams from their shells, keeping the remaining clams in their shells. Discard any clams that have not opened.

2 Heat the olive oil in a saucepan, add the chopped garlic and cook gently until golden but not brown. Add the courgettes, lemon rind and marjoram and turn them in the oil and garlic. Pour in the stock, season lightly with salt and pepper and bring to simmering point. Cover the pan and simmer for about 10 minutes or until the courgettes are soft.

3 Pass the soup through a coarse food mill and return it to the pan. Add the reserved clam juice and the shelled clams. If the soup is too thick, add extra stock or water. Taste and season with salt and pepper and a little lemon juice. Stir in the clams in their shells.

4 To serve, rub the toasted bread with the bruised garlic clove, place a slice in each bowl and ladle on the soup. Drizzle each serving with olive oil and serve immediately.

Iced Tomato and Pepper Soup with Salsa Verde

This soup relies on full-flavoured, sun-ripened tomatoes to conjure up the taste of southern Italy. Adding the salsa verde gives the soup a sweet and sour flavour, popular in the south of Italy and Sicily. The salsa will keep for up to 1 week in the refrigerator.

Serves: **6**

Preparation time: 20 minutes, plus chilling

1 kg/2 lb fresh, vine-ripened red tomatoes, or good quality canned chopped tomatoes

2 large red peppers, halved, cored and deseeded

2 garlic cloves, chopped

1 small red chilli, deseeded and finely chopped

600 ml/1 pint Mediterranean tomato juice or passata (strained crushed tomatoes)

6 tablespoons extra virgin olive oil

2 tablespoons balsamic vinegar

salt and pepper

600 ml/1 pint crushed ice, to serve

SALSA VERDE

2 garlic cloves, finely chopped

4 anchovy fillets in oil, rinsed and chopped

3 tablespoons each chopped parsley, mint and basil

2 tablespoons salted capers, rinsed and chopped

150 ml/¼ pint extra virgin olive oil, plus extra to seal

2 tablespoons lemon juice

1 Remove the cores from the tomatoes with a small sharp knife. Plunge the tomatoes into boiling water for 5–10 seconds, then remove them and refresh in cold water. Slip off the skins. Cut them in half around the middle and gently squeeze out and discard the seeds. Put the tomatoes into a food processor.

2 Roughly chop the red peppers and add to the tomatoes with the garlic and chopped chilli. Blend to a rough purée. Transfer the purée to a bowl and stir in the tomato juice or passata, olive oil and balsamic vinegar to taste. Season with salt and pepper, then cover and chill overnight to allow the flavours to develop.

3 Meanwhile, make the salsa verde. Pound 1 teaspoon salt with the garlic until creamy, using a pestle and mortar. Tip it into a bowl and stir in the anchovies, herbs, capers, olive oil and lemon juice and season with pepper. Transfer to a jar and pour a layer of olive oil on top to exclude the air.

4 To serve, stir the crushed ice into the soup and serve the salsa verde separately in a bowl to stir into the soup.

Antipasti, Bruschetta and Crostini

Deep-fried Sage Leaves

These sage leaves may seem a last moment fiddle, but they are the most delicious appetizer to have with drinks. They can be dipped singly in batter and fried, or sandwiched together with a paste of anchovy and capers first.

Serves: **6–8**

Preparation time: 10 minutes

Cooking time: 30 seconds

24 large sage leaves
1 teaspoon salted capers, rinsed
1 tablespoon anchovy paste
oil, for deep-frying
BATTER
1 egg
150 ml/¼ pint iced water
125 g/4 oz plain white flour

1 Wash and dry the sage leaves. Mash the capers with the anchovy paste and spread on to the darker green side of 12 of the sage leaves. Press a second leaf on top to form a sandwich.

2 To make the batter, lightly whisk together the egg and iced water. Add the flour and whisk it into the egg and water mixture, leaving it a bit lumpy. Do not let it stand.

3 Heat the oil in a deep pan or wok until a piece of stale bread turns golden in a few seconds. Holding the sage leaves by the stem, dip them into the batter and lightly shake off the excess. Drop them into the hot oil, a few at a time, and fry until crisp and barely golden. This will only take a few seconds. Drain the sage leaves on kitchen paper and serve straight away.

Balsamic Figs Grilled with Prosciutto

This is an easy and quick starter to cook on the barbecue. The balsamic vinegar caramelizes on the figs, giving a sweet and sour flavour.

Serves: **4**

Preparation time: 10 minutes

Cooking time: 5 minutes

8 fresh ripe figs
2 tablespoons balsamic vinegar
2 tablespoons extra virgin olive oil, plus extra
  to serve
12 slices of prosciutto
TO SERVE
Parmesan cheese shavings
crushed black pepper

1 Take the figs one at a time and stand them upright. Using a sharp knife, make 2 cuts through each fig not quite quartering them, but keeping them intact. Ease the figs open and brush with the balsamic vinegar and olive oil.

2 Place the figs cut-side down on a preheated barbecue or griddle pan and cook for 3–4 minutes until hot and slightly charred. Alternatively, place the figs cut-side up under a hot grill until browned and heated through.

3 While the figs are cooking, place half of the slices of prosciutto on the barbecue or griddle and cook until frazzled and starting to crisp. Remove and keep warm while cooking the remaining prosciutto.

4 To serve, arrange 3 pieces of prosciutto and 2 figs each on 4 warmed plates. Cover with Parmesan shavings, drizzle with a little more olive oil and sprinkle with plenty of crushed black pepper.

Marinated Peppers with Artichokes and Anchovies

The sweet and savoury flavours of this dish combine to make it a wonderful appetizer.

Serves: **6**

Preparation time: 25 minutes, plus marinating

Cooking time: 15 minutes

6 red, orange or yellow peppers
12 artichoke hearts in oil, drained
24 anchovy fillets in oil, drained
4 garlic cloves, sliced
2 tablespoons chopped oregano
extra virgin olive oil, for drizzling
2 hard-boiled eggs, finely chopped
salt and pepper

1 Place the whole peppers in a grill pan and cook under a preheated hot grill or on a barbecue, until the skins begin to char. Turn the peppers until they are charred all over. Don't be tempted to halve the peppers to grill them or they will lose all their juices.

2 Place the peppers in a plastic bag and leave for 10 minutes to steam. Peel off the skins, then cut the peppers in half lengthways through the stalks and remove the seeds. Place the peppers cut-side up in a shallow dish.

3 Cut the artichokes in half and place 2 halves in each pepper half. Lay 2 anchovy fillets over the artichokes. Season well with salt and pepper. Scatter over the sliced garlic and chopped oregano.

4 Drizzle the peppers with olive oil. Cover and refrigerate overnight for the flavours to develop. Serve at room temperature sprinkled with the chopped hard-boiled eggs.

VARIATION • Although they are not so attractive to look at, salted anchovies have a better flavour than canned ones. They are usually sold whole and have to be rinsed, split open, and the backbone and other small bones removed before use.

Baked Ricotta Cheeses with Bay Leaves

These little savoury cheesecakes are permeated with the musky perfume of fresh bay leaves, a much-loved flavouring in Sicily. Choose soft young leaves that will bend to fit your moulds – the smell as they bake is wonderful. Serve at room temperature with just a drizzle of olive oil and some freshly ground black pepper.

Serves: **6**

Preparation time: 20 minutes, plus chilling

Cooking time: 20 minutes

Oven temperature: 190°C/375°F/Gas Mark 5

4 sun-dried tomatoes (the dried variety)
500 g/1 lb drained ricotta cheese
3 large eggs
12 oven-dried or Greek-style black olives, pitted and roughly chopped
2 tablespoons salted capers, rinsed and chopped, plus extra to garnish
a little butter
18 fresh young bay leaves
salt and pepper
TO SERVE
olive oil
rocket leaves

1 Soak the sun-dried tomatoes in warm water for 10 minutes. Pat dry and shred finely.

2 Push the ricotta through a sieve into a bowl. Beat in the eggs, then lightly stir in the sun-dried tomatoes, olives and capers. Taste and season very well.

3 Generously butter six 125 ml/4 fl oz ramekins or moulds. Place a bay leaf at the bottom of each one, and two around the sides. Chill the ramekins to set the butter and keep the bay leaves in place. Spoon in the ricotta mixture and level it with a palette knife. Set the ramekins on a baking sheet.

4 Bake the cheeses in a preheated oven, 190°C/375°F/Gas Mark 5, for 20 minutes until set. Remove them from the oven, leave to cool, then chill. Turn out the cheeses and serve at room temperature with a drizzle of olive oil, a few rocket leaves and some extra capers. The bay leaves should not be eaten.

FOOD FACT • Ricotta is a bland milky cheese, which may be made from either ewes' or cows' milk. The word *ricotta* means, literally, 'recooked' because the cheese is made from milk that has been twice heated.

Carpaccio of Fresh Tuna

When tuna is really fresh, it is almost a waste to cook it at all. Here it is chilled or lightly frozen and sliced paper thin, moistened with a lemon and oil dressing and scattered with rocket and Parmesan shavings.

Serves: **4**

Preparation time: 10 minutes, plus freezing

250 g/8 oz piece of tuna loin
12 tablespoons lemon juice
150 ml/¼ pint extra virgin olive oil
1 garlic clove, finely chopped
1 tablespoon salted capers, rinsed
125 g/4 oz rocket
salt and pepper
Parmesan shavings, to serve

1 Trim the tuna of any membrane or gristle. Wrap tightly in clingfilm and place in the freezer for about 1 hour until just frozen but not rock solid.

2 Meanwhile, whisk together the lemon juice, olive oil, garlic and capers. Add salt and pepper to taste and whisk until emulsified.

3 Unwrap the tuna and slice it thinly with a sharp, thin-bladed knife. Arrange the slices on 4 large dinner plates. Spoon the dressing over the tuna. Top with a tangle of rocket leaves and scatter with Parmesan shavings.

FOOD FACT • The caper plant grows wild all over the Mediterranean, and what we know as capers are in fact the flower buds. Capers can be cultivated but most people think the wild ones are the best. They can be bought either salted or packed in vinegar.

Griddled Asparagus with Frazzled Eggs and Parmesan

Fresh young asparagus tastes wonderful with eggs in any form. These eggs are fried in very hot olive oil, which gives them a crisp, brown lacy edge but a soft yolk.

Serves: **4**

Preparation time: 10 minutes

Cooking time: 10 minutes

500 g/1 lb asparagus, trimmed
olive oil, for frying
4 fresh eggs, chilled
salt and pepper
Parmesan shavings, to serve

1 Blanch the asparagus for 2 minutes in salted boiling water. Drain and refresh under cold water. Drain again and toss in a little olive oil, to coat.

2 Grill the asparagus on a preheated barbecue or griddle for 2–3 minutes on each side until tender but still with a bite. Set aside to cool slightly.

3 Pour enough olive oil into a large frying pan to coat the base generously and heat until almost smoking. Crack each egg into a cup and carefully slide into the pan. Watch out as the oil will splutter! Once the edges of the eggs have bubbled up and browned, turn the heat right down and cover the pan with a lid. Leave for about 1 minute, then lift out the eggs and drain them on kitchen paper. The yolks should have formed a skin, but should remain runny underneath.

4 Divide the asparagus between 4 warmed plates and top each pile with an egg. Scatter with black pepper and Parmesan shavings. Serve with a little pot of salt for the eggs.

Tuscan Chicken Liver Crostini

These crostini, which are easy to make, are served everywhere in Tuscany and there are endless variations. In Italy chicken livers are firm and plump, so try to buy fresh ones rather than frozen for this recipe. Vin santo is a Tuscan dessert wine, and adds depth of flavour to the chicken livers.

Serves: **4 generously**

Preparation time: 15 minutes

Cooking time: 15 minutes

Oven temperature: 190°C/375°F/Gas Mark 5

1 Italian sfilatino or small thin French baguette
3 tablespoons extra virgin olive oil, plus extra
  for brushing
75 g/3 oz butter
2 shallots, finely chopped
1 celery stick, finely chopped
1 small carrot, finely chopped
175 g/6 oz fresh chicken livers, trimmed and
  roughly chopped
2 tablespoons vin santo, dry sherry or white
  wine
1 tablespoon sun-dried tomato purée
2 tablespoons salted capers, rinsed and
  chopped
3 tablespoons chopped parsley
salt and pepper

1 Slice the bread into thin rounds, brush them with olive oil and arrange on a baking sheet. Bake in a preheated oven, 190°C/375°F/Gas Mark 5, for about 10 minutes until golden and crisp.

2 Heat the oil with half of the butter and gently fry the shallots, celery and carrot until softening. Stir in the livers and raise the heat to brown them lightly. Stir in the vin santo and tomato purée then turn down the heat and simmer for 15 minutes, until the liquid has all but evaporated.

3 Mix in the capers, the remaining butter, parsley and salt and pepper to taste. The mixture should look quite rough, but mash it if you like a smoother finish. Pile the topping on to the crostini and serve immediately whilst still warm or leave to cool and serve cold. Don't let the crostini get soggy.

Olive Oil

Olive oil, which has come to be known affectionately as the liquid gold of the Mediterranean, is an essential ingredient in Italian cooking and no kitchen is complete without it. It is needed for hundreds of different culinary tasks – be it for gently frying onion at the start of a sauce, for brushing on fish before grilling or for a salad dressing. The best oil is reputed to come from green Tuscan olives, which are harvested in early November. Lucca oil, which has an intensely peppery flavour, holds the reputation for the best of all Tuscan oils.

Olives are the small oval fruits of the olive tree, which originated in the East. Large quantities of olives were eaten by both the ancient Greeks and the ancient Egyptians, who believed that the goddess Isis had discovered how to extract the oil. In Greek mythology, Pallas Athene struck the Acropolis with her spear and out sprang the olive tree. She is then supposed to have taught men how to cultivate it and how to use its fruits.

The ancient Romans also venerated the olive tree for its essential role in nutrition and food preparation. It was they who are reputed to have brought the olive tree to the Mediterranean region, together with the techniques of olive oil extraction, where it is now widely cultivated.

Olive oil production

Nowadays, 95 per cent of the world production of olives is used for the extraction of oil. The basic method of oil production has hardly changed since the Etruscans started production thousands of years ago, though the detail of the method and the equipment have been much improved. The olives are picked, mostly by hand, very carefully so as not to bruise them, and the whole olives, including the stones, are then coarsely crushed. They are then placed in heavy folding mats and pressed, which is usually done nowadays with a hydraulic press. The resultant oil and the watery juice are drained off and separated, and the oil is filtered.

Olive oil has long been regarded as the finest oil for all culinary purposes. It varies substantially in flavour, according to the variety of olive used, and is also affected by the terrain, climate and age of the olive. In general, oil that is pressed from young green olives tends to have a fresh fruity taste, while that which is pressed from mature black olives tends to be richer, greener and stronger.

It varies, too, in quality, depending on exactly how and when the oil was extracted, and is graded, in line with rules laid down by the International Olive Oil Council, according to its acidity content. The best oils are extracted under pressure from ripe, or partially ripe, olives, without the addition of any water or chemicals.

Extra virgin olive oil

Extra virgin olive oil is the finest quality oil and consequently the most expensive you can buy. It is the result of the first pressing of the olives, after separating and filtering, and is sometimes also referred to as 'first cold pressed' or 'cold drawn'. It is a straightforward, honest product, which is unadulterated, untampered with and absolutely pure. It has a rich, fruity, full-bodied aroma and flavour and a rich, green colour. Extra virgin olive oil has an acidity level of up to 1 per cent (the lower the acidity level, the better the quality and the more aromatic the oil).

Virgin olive oil

Virgin olive oil is the second pressing. It has cold water added to the remaining pulp after the first pressing and is also sometimes referred to as 'fine', 'superfine' or 'extra fine' oil. It has a slightly sharper flavour and an acidity of up to 1.5 per cent.

Pure olive oil

Pure olive oil comes from a further pressing. It has a correspondingly paler colour and its flavour is coarser and has less character to it. This type of oil is also referred to as 'semi-fine' virgin olive oil or just as 'olive oil', and has an acidity of up to 3 per cent. It may sometimes be a mixture of unrefined and refined oils blended together.

Refined oils

Refined oils are those that do not make it through to the top three grades mentioned above and are stripped of flavour by chemical processes. They will usually have some hint of flavour returned to them by mixing with a little virgin olive oil.

Choosing olive oil

The choice of oil depends on its use in cooking. Extra virgin oils have a strong full flavour, which is only really suitable for big bold dishes that benefit from this strength of flavour, such as pesto, meat marinades, roasted vegetables, salads and pasta sauces. For more delicate dishes, such as fish dishes, where you don't want the flavour of the ingredients to be overwhelmed by that of the oil, use a lighter oil.

If you are not used to olive oil, it is probably best to start with a non-virgin olive oil, which will have a light flavour; then, as you develop a taste for it, you can progress to virgin and extra virgin. After that, there will be no looking back.

Olive oil is unsuitable for deep frying as it cannot tolerate the high temperatures that are required.

Storing

Olive oil can turn rancid if it is exposed to too much air or light. Store it in a cool dark cupboard and, after opening, refrigerate it or transfer to smaller containers for 6–10 months. Refrigeration can cause the oil to cloud, but it will clear when returned to room temperature.

Flavoured oils

Herb-flavoured oils can be made by combining your favourite herbs, such as rosemary, basil, chives or mint, with olive oil. Put 4 tablespoons of your preferred chopped herb with 450 ml/ ¾ pint of olive oil in a sealed jar or bottle. Leave to infuse for about 10 days, shaking occasionally. Strain the oil into a bottle with a screw top, add a sprig of the fresh herb and seal the bottle. It will keep f or up to 3 months.

Other flavoured oils include citrus oil, which is made by infusing finely chopped oranges or lemons in the oil for 2 hours before straining it. Chilli oil can be made using fresh or dried chillies, which you heat in the oil for a few seconds before cooling and straining. Citrus and chilli oils should be used within a week.

Black Olive, Pine Nut, Caper and Tuna Crostini

These crostini embody all the flavours of the hot south on a crunchy base.

Serves: **6**

Preparation time: 10 minutes

Cooking time: 10 minutes

Oven temperature: 190°C/375°F/Gas Mark 5

1 Italian sfilatino or small thin French baguette
extra virgin olive oil, for brushing
175 g/6 oz oven-baked or Greek-style black
  olives, pitted and roughly chopped
1 tablespoon salted capers, rinsed and chopped
2 tablespoons pine nuts, roughly chopped
1 small garlic clove, finely chopped
1 tablespoon chopped parsley
6 sun-dried tomatoes (the dried variety), soaked
  and roughly chopped
1 tablespoon finely grated lemon rind
100 g/3½ oz can tuna in oil, drained
salt and pepper

1 Slice the bread into thin rounds, brush them with olive oil and arrange on a baking sheet. Bake in a preheated oven, 190°C/375°F/Gas Mark 5, for about 10 minutes until golden and crisp.

2 Combine the olives, capers, pine nuts, garlic, parsley, sun-dried tomatoes and lemon rind in a bowl. Work in the tuna so that it breaks up and amalgamates with the other ingredients. Moisten with a little olive oil, taste, season with salt and pepper and pile on top of the crostini.

FOOD FACT • Pine nuts, or pine kernels, are the small, tear-drop-shaped nuts of the pine tree. They have a soft texture and a buttery sweetness that make them an excellent addition to many sweet and savoury dishes. They have a limited shelf life and will turn rancid, so make sure you use them quickly.

VARIATION • If you prefer a sharper flavour, use a mixture of green and black olives.

Broad Bean, Pear and Pecorino Crostini

In the spring, mounds of fresh young broad beans are on sale everywhere in Italy and are eaten as a snack or starter with sliced Pecorino cheese.

Serves: **6**

Preparation time: 15 minutes

Cooking time: 10 minutes

Oven temperature: 190°C/375°F/Gas Mark 5

1 Italian sfilatino or small thin French baguette
extra virgin olive oil, for brushing
250 g/8 oz shelled fresh broad beans
1 small ripe pear, peeled, cored and finely
  chopped
drop of balsamic or sherry vinegar
125 g/4 oz Pecorino cheese, salted ricotta
  or feta
salt and pepper

1 Slice the bread into thin rounds, brush them with olive oil and arrange on a baking sheet. Bake in a preheated oven, 190°C/375°F/Gas Mark 5, for about 10 minutes until golden and crisp.

2 Blanch the beans for 3 minutes in boiling water. Drain them and refresh in cold water. Pop them out of their skins. Roughly mash them with a fork, moisten with a little olive oil and season well with salt and pepper.

3 Mix the chopped pear with a drop of balsamic vinegar. Cut the cheese into small cubes and mix with the pear and vinegar.

4 Spread each crostini with a mound of bean purée and top with a spoonful of the pear and cheese mixture. Serve immediately.

FOOD FACT • Broad beans can be fresh, frozen or canned, and go particularly well with Pecorino cheese. Tiny garden-fresh beans are the best, and if you can take the time to skin them, this is well worth the effort.

Slow-roasted Tomatoes on Bruschetta

These firm but juicy tomatoes burst with the flavour of the sun. They take no time to prepare but spend a long time in the oven and smell fantastic while cooking. You can use other vine-ripened varieties if you like – just make sure that they have plenty of flavour.

Serves: **4**

Preparation time: 10 minutes

Cooking time: 2 hours

Oven temperature: 160°C/325°F/Gas Mark 3

4 large vine-ripened plum tomatoes
2 garlic cloves, finely chopped
1 tablespoon dried oregano
4 tablespoons extra virgin olive oil, plus extra
    for drizzling
50 g/2 oz salted ricotta or feta cheese, cut into
    slivers
salt and pepper
basil leaves, to garnish
BRUSCHETTA
4 thick slices of country bread
2 garlic cloves, bruised

1 Cut the tomatoes in half lengthways. Put them cut-side up on a baking sheet.

2 Mix the garlic and oregano with the olive oil and salt and pepper to taste. Spoon or brush this mixture over the cut tomatoes and bake them in a preheated oven, 160°C/325°F/Gas Mark 3, for about 2 hours, checking every now and then. The tomatoes should be slightly shrunk but still a brilliant red colour. If they are too dark, they will be bitter. Remove the tomatoes from the oven and leave to cool.

3 Barbecue, toast or griddle the bread on both sides then rub each slice with the bruised garlic and drizzle with olive oil. Cut the bruschetta slices so that 2 tomato halves will sit comfortably on each one. Cover the tomatoes with the cheese slivers and top with a basil leaf. Serve at room temperature.

FOOD FACT • Feta cheese is, in fact, Greek but it makes a good alternative to ricotta if the latter is not available.

Tomato and Bocconcini Bruschetta

True bruschetta is a large slice of country bread toasted on a barbecue or over a wood fire, rubbed with garlic and sometimes topped with a crushed tomato, at most. It is a popular snack all over Italy, served both in bars and at home. This is a slightly more sophisticated version of the original.

Serves: **4**

Preparation time: 10 minutes

Cooking time: 5 minutes

3 tablespoons extra virgin olive oil, plus extra
  for drizzling
1 teaspoon balsamic vinegar
12 bocconcini (baby mozzarella), halved, or
  375 g/12 oz mozzarella, cut into cubes
20 baby plum tomatoes or ripe cherry
  tomatoes, halved
2 tablespoons chopped basil
4 thick slices of country bread
2 garlic cloves, bruised
125 g/4 oz rocket
salt and pepper
basil leaves, to garnish

1 Whisk the olive oil and balsamic vinegar with salt and pepper to taste. Stir in the halved bocconcini, tomatoes and basil.

2 Barbecue, toast or griddle the bread on both sides, rub each slice with the bruised garlic and drizzle with olive oil.

3 Cover each slice of toasted bread with a few rocket leaves and spoon over some of the tomato and mozzarella mixture. Drizzle with extra olive oil and garnish with basil leaves.

Shaved Porcini Bruschetta with Truffle Oil

The porcini season is short, so make the most of this elusive fruit of the forest by showing it off to its best advantage.

Serves: **4**

Preparation time: 15 minutes

Cooking time: 5 minutes

4 thick slices of country bread
2 garlic cloves, bruised
extra virgin olive oil, for drizzling
2 tablespoons chopped parsley
4 small fresh porcini (ceps)
lemon juice, for drizzling
truffle oil, for drizzling
salt and pepper

1 Barbecue, toast or griddle the bread on both sides and rub each slice with the bruised garlic. Drizzle the slices with olive oil and sprinkle with parsley.

2 Pick over the mushrooms and brush off any grit. Remove the stems and slice them finely. Slice the caps as finely as possible.

3 Cut the bruschetta slices in half. Strew them with the sliced porcini stems and sprinkle with a little lemon juice and salt and pepper. Cover with the sliced caps. Drizzle with more lemon juice and a little truffle oil and season with black pepper. Serve immediately.

FOOD FACT • Truffle oil is available from Italian delicatessens. It is not cheap, but a little goes a long way so it is economical to use.

Risotto

Parmesan and Butter Risotto

Serves: **6**

Preparation time: 10 minutes

Cooking time: 30 minutes

125 g/4 oz butter
1 large onion, finely chopped
150 ml/¼ pint dry white wine
500 g/1 lb risotto rice
pinch of saffron threads
1.5 litres/2½ pints hot Chicken or Vegetable
   Stock (see pages 8 and 9)
75 g/3 oz freshly grated Parmesan cheese
salt and pepper

1 Melt half of the butter in a large saucepan and add the onion. Cook gently for 10 minutes until soft and golden but not coloured. Pour in the wine and boil hard until it has reduced and almost disappeared.

2 Pour in the rice, add the saffron and stir until well coated with butter and heated through. Add the stock, a large ladleful at a time, and stir until each ladleful is absorbed into the rice. Continue adding stock and cooking until the rice is tender and creamy, but the grains are still firm. This should take about 20 minutes depending on the type of rice used. Taste and season well with salt and pepper then stir in the remaining butter and the Parmesan.

3 Cover the pan and leave the risotto to rest for a few minutes, then serve.

FOOD FACT • Saffron is the most expensive spice in the world, but it is also one of the most potent, so a little imparts a lot of flavour.

Pumpkin, Sage and Chilli Risotto

Serves: **6**

Preparation time: 20 minutes

Cooking time: 30 minutes

125 g/4 oz butter
1 large onion, finely chopped
1–2 fresh or dried red chillies, deseeded and
  finely chopped
500 g/1 lb pumpkin, peeled and roughly
  chopped
500 g/1 lb risotto rice
1.5 litres/2½ pints hot Chicken or Vegetable
  Stock (see pages 8 and 9)
3 tablespoons chopped sage
75 g/3 oz freshly grated Parmesan cheese
salt and pepper
sage sprigs, to garnish

1 Heat half of the butter in a large saucepan
and add the onion. Cook gently for 10 minutes
until softened but not coloured. Stir in the red
chillies and cook for 1 minute. Add the
pumpkin and cook, stirring constantly over the
heat, for 5 minutes.

2 Stir in the rice to coat it with the butter and
vegetables. Cook for a couple of minutes to
toast the grains. Add the stock, a large ladleful
at a time, stirring until each ladleful is
absorbed into the rice. Continue adding stock
and cooking until the rice is tender and
creamy but the grains are still firm and the
pumpkin is beginning to disintegrate. This
should take about 20 minutes depending on
the type of rice used. Taste and season well
with salt and pepper then stir in the sage, the
remaining butter and the Parmesan.

3 Cover the pan and leave the risotto to rest
for a few minutes, then serve garnished with
sage sprigs.

Wild Mushroom Risotto

Serves: **6**

Preparation time: 20 minutes

Cooking time: 30 minutes

125 g/4 oz butter or oil
1 large onion, finely chopped
2 garlic cloves, finely chopped
175 g/6 oz mixed wild mushrooms or porcini
   (or the equivalent in dried mushrooms),
   roughly chopped
1 tablespoon chopped mixed thyme and
   marjoram
150 ml/¼ pint dry white wine
500 g/1 lb risotto rice
1.5 litres/2½ pints hot Chicken or Vegetable
   Stock (see pages 8 and 9)
salt and pepper
marjoram leaves, to garnish
75 g/3 oz freshly grated Parmesan
   cheese, to serve

1 Melt the butter or oil in a large saucepan and add the onion and garlic. Cook gently for 10 minutes until soft but not coloured. Stir in the mushrooms and herbs, and cook over a moderate heat for 3 minutes. Pour in the wine and boil hard until it has almost evaporated.

2 Stir in the rice and fry with the onion and mushrooms until slightly opaque. Add the stock, a large ladleful at a time, stirring until each ladleful is absorbed into the rice. Continue adding stock and cooking until the rice is tender and creamy, but the grains are still firm. This should take about 20 minutes depending on the type of rice used. Taste and season well with salt and pepper.

3 Cover the pan and leave the risotto to rest for a few of minutes, garnish with marjoram leaves, then serve with the grated Parmesan.

Red Wine Risotto

Serves: **6**

Preparation time: 20 minutes

Cooking time: 35 minutes

125 g/4 oz butter
1 onion, finely chopped
1 carrot, finely chopped
1 celery stick, finely chopped
50 g/2 oz pancetta, finely chopped
300 ml/½ pint red wine
500 g/1 lb risotto rice
1.5 litres/2½ pints hot Chicken or Vegetable
  Stock (see pages 8 and 9)
125 g/4 oz freshly grated Parmesan cheese, plus
  extra to garnish
salt and pepper
parsley, to garnish

1 Melt half of the butter in a large saucepan and add the onion, carrot and celery. Cook gently for 10 minutes until soft but not coloured. Add the pancetta and cook for another 5 minutes. Pour in the wine and boil hard until it has reduced by half.

2 Pour in the rice and stir until well coated with the juices and heated through. Add the stock, a large ladleful at a time, stirring until each ladleful is absorbed into the rice. Continue adding stock and cooking until the rice is tender and creamy, but the grains are still firm. This should take about 20 minutes depending on the type of rice used. Taste and season well with salt and pepper. Stir in the remaining butter and the Parmesan.

3 Cover the pan and leave the risotto to rest for a few of minutes, then serve garnished with parsley and grated Parmesan.

FOOD FACT • Pancetta is unsmoked bacon taken from the belly of a pig. It is cured with spices, salt and pepper, and is then rolled into a sausage shape and sliced thinly.

Seafood Saffron Risotto

This is a delicious wine and seafood risotto, bright yellow and fragrant with saffron. Italians do not generally serve Parmesan cheese with seafood.

Serves: **6 generously**

Preparation time: 30 minutes

Cooking time: about 1 hour

2 large pinches of saffron threads
375 g/12 oz raw shell-on prawns
1.5 litres/2½ pints Fish Stock (see page 9)
300 ml/½ pint dry white wine
6 baby squid, cleaned
6 scallops
600 ml/1 pint mussels
300 ml/½ pint small clams
75 g/3 oz butter
1 onion, finely chopped
500 g/1 lb risotto rice
3 tablespoons chopped parsley, to garnish

1 Soak the saffron threads in a small bowl of warm water.

2 Remove the heads from the prawns and put the heads into a large saucepan with the stock and wine. Bring to the boil, cover the pan and simmer for 20 minutes.

3 Cut the squid into rings and trim the tentacles. Remove the hard white muscle from the side of each scallop and separate the white flesh from the orange roe. Scrub the mussels well and pull off any beards. Discard any that do not close when sharply tapped. Rinse the clams well.

4 Strain the prawn stock into a clean saucepan and bring to simmering point. Add the prawns and cook for 2 minutes. Add the squid, scallops and their roe and cook for a further 2 minutes. Remove them all with a slotted spoon and set aside. Put the mussels and clams into the stock and bring to the boil. Cover and cook for 5 minutes or until all the shellfish have opened. Remove with a slotted spoon. Discard any that have not opened.

5 Melt the butter in a large saucepan and add the onion. Cook gently for 10 minutes until soft but not coloured. Pour in the rice and stir until well coated with butter and heated through. Add the hot stock, a large ladleful at a time, stirring until each ladleful is absorbed into the rice. Continue adding stock and cooking until all but 2 ladlefuls of stock are left, and the rice is tender but still has some bite to it. This should take about 20 minutes. Taste and season well with salt and pepper.

6 Finally stir in the remaining stock and all the seafood and cook gently with the lid on for 5 minutes or until piping hot. Transfer the risotto to a large warmed bowl and sprinkle with the parsley. Serve immediately.

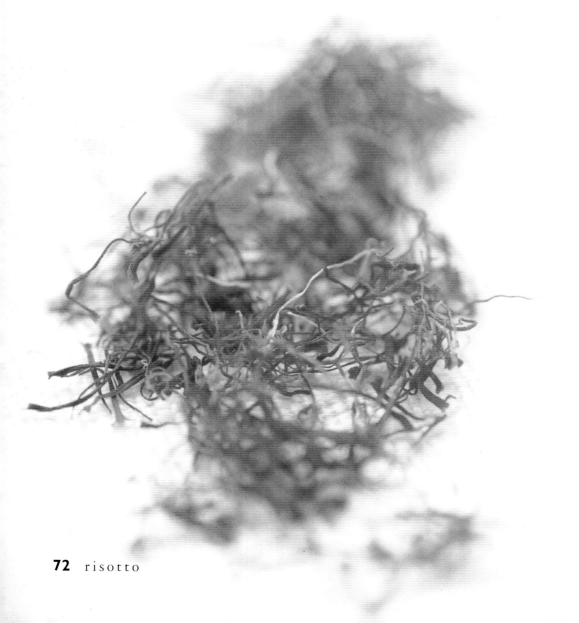

Roasted Garlic and Leek Risotto

Serves: **4**

Preparation time: 30 minutes

Cooking time: 45 minutes

6 large garlic cloves
about 150 ml/¼ pint olive oil
500 g/1 lb medium leeks, plus 2 extra to garnish
oil, for deep-frying
500 g/1 lb risotto rice
1.5 litres/2½ pints hot Chicken or Vegetable
    Stock (see pages 8 and 9)
50 g/2 oz freshly grated Parmesan cheese
salt and pepper

1 Put the garlic cloves into a small saucepan. Cover completely with the olive oil and bring to a simmer, continue to simmer for about 20 minutes or until the garlic is golden and soft. Leave the garlic to cool in the oil. Remove the garlic cloves once cool and set aside.

2 Cut the 2 leeks for the garnish into 7 cm/3 inch lengths, then slice them in half lengthways and cut into long thin shreds. Deep-fry the shredded leeks for 1–2 minutes until crisp and just golden. Lift them out of the oil with a slotted spoon and drain on kitchen paper. Slice the remaining leeks into rounds, as thinly or thickly as you like.

3 Heat 75 ml/3 fl oz of the garlic-flavoured olive oil in a heavy-based pan. Add the sliced leeks and sauté for a few minutes until they are beginning to soften and colour slightly, then stir in the garlic cloves.

4 Pour in the rice and stir until it is well coated with oil and heated through. Add the stock, a large ladleful at a time, stirring until each ladleful is absorbed into the rice. Continue adding stock and cooking until the rice is tender and creamy, but the grains are still firm. This should take about 20 minutes. Season well, stir in the Parmesan and cover the pan. Leave the risotto to rest for a few minutes before serving, garnished with a tangle of fried leeks.

Lemon and Thyme Risotto with Vodka

A wonderful light and fragrant risotto, perfect for the summer. Serve on its own or as an accompaniment to a meat or fish dish.

Serves: **6**

Preparation time: 20 minutes

Cooking time: 30 minutes

1 Melt half of the butter in a large saucepan, add the spring onions or young shallots and cook gently for 3–5 minutes until soft. Pour in the wine, add half of the lemon rind and boil hard to reduce the wine until it has almost disappeared.

2 Pour in the rice and stir until it is well coated with butter and onions and heated through. Add the hot stock, a large ladleful at a time, stirring until each ladleful is absorbed into the rice. Continue adding stock and stirring until the rice is tender and creamy, but the grains are still firm. This should take about 20 minutes depending on the type of rice used. Taste and season well with salt and lots of freshly ground black pepper. Stir in the remaining butter and lemon rind, the lemon juice, vodka, thyme and Parmesan.

3 Cover the pan and leave the risotto to rest for a few minutes, then serve garnished with thyme sprigs and strips of lemon rind.

125 g/4 oz butter
6 spring onions or young shallots, finely chopped
150 ml/¼ pint dry white wine
finely grated rind and juice of 1 large lemon
500 g/1 lb risotto rice
1.5 litres/2½ pints hot Chicken or Vegetable Stock (see pages 8 and 9)
2 tablespoons vodka
1 tablespoon chopped thyme
75 g/3 oz freshly grated Parmesan cheese
salt and pepper
TO GARNISH
thyme sprigs
strips of lemon rind

FOOD FACT • Thyme may be used either fresh or dried, though fresh has a better flavour. It goes especially well with lemon, as used here.

Creamy Radicchio Risotto

A dish from the Veneto, where risotto rice is grown as well as several varieties of radicchio. This risotto has both a sweet and a bitter flavour.

Serves: **6**

Preparation time: 15 minutes

Cooking time: 30 minutes

125 g/4 oz butter
2 carrots, finely diced
125 g/4 oz smoked pancetta, finely diced
2 garlic cloves, finely chopped
500 g/1 lb radicchio, finely shredded
500 g/1 lb risotto rice
1.5 litres/2½ pints hot Chicken or Vegetable Stock (see pages 8 and 9)
3 tablespoons single cream
75 g/3 oz freshly grated Parmesan cheese, plus extra to serve
salt and pepper

1 Melt half of the butter in a large saucepan and add the carrot. Cook gently for 5 minutes until it starts to soften. Add the pancetta and garlic and cook until just beginning to colour. Stir in the radicchio and cook until it begins to wilt.

2 Add the rice and stir until heated through. Add a ladleful of the hot stock and simmer, stirring all the time, until it has been absorbed. Continue cooking and adding the stock, a ladleful at a time, until all the stock has been absorbed. The rice should be tender and creamy but still have some bite to it. This should take about 20 minutes depending on the type of rice used. Taste and season well with salt and plenty of freshly ground black pepper then stir in the remaining butter, the cream and Parmesan.

3 Cover the pan and leave the risotto to rest for a few minutes. Serve sprinkled with a little grated Parmesan.

FOOD FACT • Radicchio is a popular salad vegetable in Italy, which may be eaten either raw or, as in this recipe, cooked without collapsing to nothing. It has an attractive colour, a pleasantly bitter flavour, and its leaves are firm.

Stuffed Riceballs

These are crisp golden balls, or suppli, *which are stuffed with a melting mixture of mozzarella, salami and basil leaves. They are delicious as substantial snacks, when made into orange-sized balls, and perfect to serve with drinks, when made into bite-sized morsels, as here.*

Makes: **20 balls**

Preparation time: 30 minutes, plus cooling

Cooking time: 45 minutes

75 g/3 oz butter
1 onion, finely chopped
150 ml/¼ pint dry white wine
275 g/9 oz risotto rice
900 ml/1½ pints hot Chicken Stock (see page 8)
25 g/1 oz freshly grated Parmesan cheese
2 small eggs
50 g/2 oz mozzarella, finely diced
50 g/2 oz salami, finely diced
20 small basil leaves
125 g/4 oz dried white breadcrumbs
oil, for deep-frying
salt and pepper

1 Melt the butter in a large saucepan and add the chopped onion. Cook gently for 10 minutes until soft and golden but not coloured. Pour in the wine and boil hard to reduce until it has almost disappeared.

2 Stir in the rice and coat with the butter and wine. Add a ladleful of stock and simmer, stirring, until it has been absorbed. Continue cooking and adding the stock, a ladleful at a time, until all the stock has been absorbed. The rice should be tender and creamy but still have some bite to it. This should take about 20 minutes. Taste and season well with salt and pepper and stir in the Parmesan. Remove from the heat and leave to cool completely.

3 Lightly whisk the eggs and beat them into the cold risotto. Take 1 tablespoon of the risotto and, with wet hands, spread it in the palm of one hand. Add a small basil leaf and a cube of mozzarella or salami. Take another tablespoon of risotto and place it over the mozzarella or salami and basil to enclose them completely. Shape into a smooth round ball. Continue until all the risotto is used up.

4 Pour the breadcrumbs into a shallow bowl and roll the rice balls in the breadcrumbs until they are evenly covered. Heat the oil in a large saucepan to 180°C/350°F or until a crumb dropped into the oil sizzles immediately. Fry the rice balls a few at a time for 3–5 minutes until golden. Drain on kitchen paper, sprinkle with a little salt and serve immediately.

VARIATION • Add saffron to the risotto for a different flavour and add chopped sun-dried tomatoes to the filling.

Pasta and Sauces

Basic Tomato Sauce

This is the perfect sauce for pizza bases, dressing pasta and enriching other sauces. Any sauce which you do not use straight away can be kept, covered, in the refrigerator for up to 1 week.

Serves: **4**

Preparation time: 10 minutes

Cooking time: 1 hour

1 kg/2 lb fresh ripe tomatoes, quartered, or
   drained canned whole tomatoes, roughly
   chopped
1 onion, finely chopped
2 garlic cloves, chopped
4 basil leaves, bruised
125 ml/4 fl oz olive oil

1 Place the tomatoes in a large saucepan with the onion and garlic. Cover the pan, bring to the boil then cook slowly for 25 minutes.

2 Uncover the pan and simmer for another 15–30 minutes to evaporate any extra liquid, as the sauce should be quite thick.

3 Purée the sauce in a blender, then sieve it to remove any seeds and skin. Stir in the basil and oil.

FOOD FACT • Fresh plum tomatoes are the best ones to use to make tomato sauce and will give the most sustained flavour, but failing that, a can of tomatoes will do almost as well.

Penne with Walnut Sauce

Serves: **4–6**

Preparation time: 15 minutes

Cooking time: 8–12 minutes

Oven temperature: 190°C/375°F/Gas Mark 5

500–750 g/1–1½ lb penne rigate
300 ml/½ pint milk
2 slices of wholemeal bread, crusts removed
300 g/10 oz walnut pieces
1 garlic clove, crushed
50 g/2 oz freshly grated Parmesan cheese, plus
   extra to garnish
100 ml/3½ fl oz olive oil
150 ml/¼ pint double cream
salt and pepper

1 Bring at least 2 litres/3½ pints of water to the boil in a large saucepan. Add a pinch of salt. Cook the pasta for 8–12 minutes or according to packet instructions.

2 Meanwhile, pour the milk into a shallow dish and soak the bread slices until all of the milk has been absorbed.

3 At the same time, spread the walnuts on a baking sheet and toast in a preheated oven, 190°C/375°F/Gas Mark 5, for 5 minutes. Set aside to cool.

4 Put the bread, walnuts, garlic, Parmesan and olive oil into a food processor and blend until smooth. Season to taste with salt and pepper, then stir in the double cream. Serve immediately tossed with the hot pasta, garnished with grated Parmesan.

FOOD FACT • For a rich dark sauce, add 125 g/4 oz pitted black oven-dried olives to the ingredients in the food processor.

Tagliatelle with Rocket and Cherry Tomato Sauce

This quick sauce uses peppery rocket as if it were spinach, stirred into garlicky sweet cherry tomatoes until wilted, then seasoned with balsamic vinegar.

Serves: **4**

Preparation time: 10 minutes

Cooking time: 8–12 minutes

500 g/1 lb tagliatelle verde
3 tablespoons olive oil
2 garlic cloves, finely chopped
500 g/1 lb very ripe cherry tomatoes, halved
1 tablespoon balsamic vinegar
175 g/6 oz rocket
salt and pepper
Parmesan cheese shavings, to serve

1 Bring at least 2 litres/3½ pints of water to the boil in a large saucepan. Add a pinch of salt. Cook the pasta for 8–12 minutes or according to packet instructions.

2 Meanwhile, heat the oil in a frying pan, add the garlic and cook for 1 minute until golden. Add the tomatoes and cook for barely 1 minute. The tomatoes should only just heat through and start to disintegrate.

3 Sprinkle the tomatoes with the balsamic vinegar, allow it to evaporate, then toss in the rocket. Carefully stir to mix it with the tomatoes and heat through so that the rocket is just wilted. Season well with salt and plenty of freshly ground black pepper. Serve immediately tossed with the hot cooked pasta and covered with plenty of Parmesan shavings.

Pesto Trapanese

This recipe is a legacy of the Arab domination of Sicily. The Arabs brought almonds to the island, and this pesto comes from Trapani, where they first settled. It really is a taste from the past, yet well suited to today's cooking. It has a very garlicky flavour.

Serves: **4–6**

Preparation time: 12 minutes

Cooking time: 8–12 minutes

500–750 g/1–1½ lb pasta twists, eg. fusilli
3 ripe tomatoes
4 garlic cloves
50 g/2 oz basil leaves, plus extra to garnish
125 g/4 oz blanched almonds, toasted
150 ml/¼ pint olive oil
salt and pepper

1 Bring at least 2 litres/3½ pints of water to the boil in a large saucepan. Add a pinch of salt. Cook the pasta for 8–12 minutes or according to packet instructions.

2 Meanwhile, place all the remaining ingredients in a food processor and blend until smooth. Alternatively, finely chop the tomatoes, garlic, basil and almonds by hand, and stir in the olive oil to give a chunkier sauce. Season to taste with salt and pepper.

3 Toss the pesto with the cooked pasta. The pesto is warmed by the heat of the pasta. Garnish with a few basil leaves.

4 The pesto can be prepared in advance, if liked. Once prepared, spoon the pesto into a jar, pour a layer of olive oil over the surface and chill until required. To use this sauce, let it come to room temperature then stir it into freshly cooked pasta.

Pappardelle with Hare Sauce

This is a really rich wintry sauce, redolent of Tuscany.

Serves: **4**

Preparation time: 30 minutes

Cooking time: 2 hours 20 minutes

1 hare or rabbit, skinned and jointed
3 tablespoons olive oil
50 g/2 oz butter
1 onion, finely diced
1 carrot, finely diced
1 celery stick, finely diced
2 garlic cloves, chopped
75 g/3 oz unsmoked pancetta, diced
2 tablespoons flour
300 ml/½ pint dry red wine
about 600 ml/1 pint Chicken Stock
  (see page 8)
1 teaspoon chopped rosemary
1 tablespoon chopped sage
2 bay leaves
500 g/1 lb pappardelle or other wide noodles
melted butter, to toss
salt and pepper

1 Cut all the meat off the hare or rabbit with a sharp knife, then cut it into small dice.

2 Heat the oil and butter in a sauté pan and add the diced onion, carrot, celery and garlic. Stir well and cook gently for about 10 minutes until soft and beginning to brown.

3 Add the pancetta and hare or rabbit, stir well and cook for a couple of minutes until the meat is browned. Season well with salt and pepper. Stir in the flour, then the wine and half of the stock. Mix well, scraping up any sediment from the bottom of the pan. Add the rosemary, sage and bay leaves and bring to the boil. Turn down the heat, half cover the pan and simmer gently for at least 2 hours, topping up with more stock as necessary, until the meat is very tender and the sauce thick and reduced.

4 Meanwhile, bring at least 2 litres/3½ pints of water to the boil in a large saucepan. Add a pinch of salt. Cook the pasta for 8–12 minutes or according to packet instructions. Drain and toss with a generous amount of melted butter.

5 Taste the sauce, season as necessary and remove the bay leaves from the pan. Toss the sauce with the buttered pappardelle. This sauce is sometimes liquidized to make it finer.

VARIATION • To make a much lighter sauce, use a jointed rabbit instead of a hare.

Carter's Pasta

This pasta was a staple food of Sicilian cart drivers, quickly rustled up by the side of the road with a few basic ingredients – tomatoes, garlic, olive oil, spaghetti and salted ricotta, which kept well because it was preserved. The recipe has been refined somewhat to suit modern, indoor kitchens.

Serves: **6**

Preparation time: 15 minutes

Cooking time: 8–12 minutes

750 g/1½ lb dried spaghetti
6 ripe tomatoes, about 750 g/1½ lb
4–5 garlic cloves, peeled
50 g/2 oz basil leaves
pinch of dried chilli flakes
150 ml/¼ pint olive oil
125 g/4 oz salted ricotta or pecorino cheese, grated, plus extra to serve
salt

1 Bring at least 2 litres/3½ pints of water to the boil in a large saucepan. Add a pinch of salt. Cook the pasta for 8–12 minutes or according to packet instructions.

2 Meanwhile, peel and chop the tomatoes, retaining all the juice, and transfer them to a bowl.

3 Put the garlic, basil, chilli flakes and a pinch of salt into a food processor and work until smooth, then add the oil slowly until the sauce becomes smooth again. Alternatively, use a pestle and mortar. Mix the purée into the chopped tomatoes.

4 Drain the pasta, reserving a couple of spoonfuls of the cooking water. Tip the spaghetti into a serving bowl, toss with half of the cheese and the cooking liquid, then mix in the sauce. Sprinkle with the remaining cheese. Serve with a small bowl of grated cheese handed separately.

Spaghetti with Garlic, Oil and Chilli

This is a classic dish which was originally from Rome but it is now popular throughout Italy. It is quick and filling. It was originally the food of the poor, since it involves nothing more extravagant than pasta, garlic and olive oil.

Serves: **4–6**

Preparation time: 5 minutes

Cooking time: 8–12 minutes

500–750 g/1–1½ lb spaghetti or spaghettini
125 ml/4 fl oz olive oil
2 garlic cloves, finely chopped
2 small dried chillies, deseeded and chopped
2 tablespoons chopped parsley
salt and pepper

1 Bring at least 2 litres/3½ pints of water to the boil in a large saucepan. Add a pinch of salt. Cook the pasta for 8–12 minutes or according to packet instructions.

2 Meanwhile, heat the olive oil in a saucepan and add the garlic and a pinch of salt. Cook gently, stirring all the time until the garlic is golden. If the garlic becomes too brown, it will taste bitter. Stir in the chillies.

3 Toss the pasta with the warm but not sizzling garlic, oil and chilli. Add plenty of black pepper and the parsley. Serve immediately.

FOOD FACT • Spaghettini is a thinner version of spaghetti which takes correspondingly less time to cook.

Homemade Pasta

Comparing dried pasta with fresh pasta is rather like comparing chalk with cheese. That's not to say that dried pasta isn't perfectly good most of the time – in fact it's delicious and every storecupboard should have a supply of it in all your favourite shapes – but fresh pasta is even better. It has a better flavour, a better texture and it takes no time at all to cook.

A lot of specialist Italian stores, delicatessens and good supermarkets stock fresh pasta, so it's easy to come by. But making your own excellent pasta dough at home is surprisingly easy, with or without a pasta machine, and is sure to impress your friends. If you have a pasta machine, this will give you a more uniform result.

Ideally, fresh pasta should be eaten on the day that it is made or purchased, though it can be refrigerated, if needs be, for up to 24 hours or frozen for up to 3 months.

Fresh egg pasta

The quantities given here are only rough guidelines and you may have to add more flour, depending on the humidity and the type of flour you use. Be careful, though – too much extra flour will make the pasta tough and taste floury. The dough must not be too soft – in fact, it should be fairly hard to knead. The serving number is similarly approximate and will depend on the size of the portions.

Serves: **2–4**

Preparation time: 15 minutes, plus resting

200 g/7 oz plain white flour (Italian 00,
   if possible)
pinch of salt
2 large eggs
1 tablespoon olive oil

1 Sift the flour and salt directly on to a clean work surface and make a well in the centre with your fist.

2 Beat together the eggs and oil, and pour these into the well.

3 Gradually mix the eggs into the flour with the fingers of one hand, and bring it together to form a dough.

4 Alternatively, you can make the pasta using a food processor. To do this, sift the flour and salt into the bowl, then pour in the beaten eggs, oil and any chosen flavouring (see below) and process the mixture until the dough begins to come together.

5 Knead the pasta until smooth. Wrap it in clingfilm and leave to rest for at least 30 minutes before attempting to roll it out. Allowing the pasta to rest will ensure that the dough is much more elastic.

There are several variations on the basic pasta dough, which will yield more interesting and flavourful results.

Spinach pasta

Proceed as for the basic pasta dough, sifting 200 g/7 oz plain white flour on to a clean work surface. (This weight is approximate and you may need a little more flour to make a firm dough.) Make a well in the centre of the flour with your fist. Cook 150 g/5 oz frozen leaf spinach and squeeze out as much of the moisture as possible. Put it into a food processor with a pinch of salt and 2 eggs, and work to a purée. Pour this into the well and continue as for the basic recipe.

Tomato pasta

Add 2 tablespoons tomato purée or sun-dried tomato paste to the flour. Use about 1½ eggs.

Beetroot pasta

Add 2 tablespoons grated cooked beetroot to the flour. Use fewer or smaller eggs.

Saffron pasta

Soak a sachet of powdered saffron in 2 tablespoons hot water for 15 minutes. Use 1½ eggs and gradually whisk the saffron water into them.

Herb pasta

Add 3 tablespoons chopped fresh herbs, for example basil, to the flour.

Black pasta

Add 1 sachet of squid ink to the eggs before adding them to the flour. A little extra flour may be needed.

Using a pasta machine

1 Feed the rested dough several times through the widest setting, folding it in three each time. Then pass the pasta through the machine again, reducing the settings until you reach the required thickness. Generally, the second from last setting is best for tagliatelle, the finest being for ravioli or for pasta that is to be filled.

2 Once the required thickness is reached, hang the pasta over a special purpose wooden pasta stand or, failing that, a broom handle, to dry a little – this will make cutting it easier as it will not be so sticky. Ravioli, on the other hand, should be made straight away, as it needs to be slightly sticky in order to adhere properly.

3 Pass the pasta through the chosen cutters and transfer it to a tray covered with a clean tea towel sprinkled with a little plain flour or semolina flour. Toss the pasta lightly in the flour and cook as soon as possible. Alternatively, drape the pasta over the pasta stand or broom handle again until you are ready to cook.

Cooking fresh pasta

1 Throw the pasta into a large saucepan of salted boiling water and stir once or twice to prevent it sticking. A tablespoon of olive oil will help to stop the water boiling over and prevent the pasta sticking, but if you have enough water in the pan and you stir the pasta as it goes in, it shouldn't stick. Do not cover the pan, or the water will boil over. As a guide, you will need 4 litres/7 pints water and 3 tablespoons salt for every 375–500 g/12 oz–1 lb fresh pasta.

2 Quickly bring the water back to a rolling boil and stir. Boil until 'al dente', calculating the cooking time from the moment the water starts to boil again. The pasta should be just firm to the bite. It should neither have a hard centre, nor be very floppy. Fresh unfilled pasta takes 2–3 minutes (some very thin pasta will be ready as soon as the water returns to the boil). Fresh filled pasta, such as tortelloni, cappelletti or ravioli, takes between 2 and 5 minutes – you can tell that the pasta is cooked when it rises to the surface.

3 Quickly drain the pasta in a large colander or sieve. Hold back 2–3 tablespoons of the cooking water – this will help the sauce to cling to the pasta. Dress the pasta immediately with the sauce of your choice, oil or butter. Serve the hot pasta straight away. The Italian way is to toss the pasta with the sauce before serving.

Pasta with Spinach and Anchovies

Serves: **4**

Preparation time: 15 minutes

Cooking time: 8–12 minutes

1 kg/2 lb fresh spinach or 625 g/1¼ lb frozen leaf
  spinach, defrosted
500 g/1 lb angel hair pasta or spaghetti
4 tablespoons olive oil
3 tablespoons pine nuts
2 garlic cloves, crushed
6 canned anchovies, drained and chopped
3 tablespoons sultanas (optional)
salt
TO SERVE
melted butter
freshly grated Parmesan cheese

1 If using fresh spinach, wash it well and remove the tough stalks. Drain thoroughly. Put the leaves into a large saucepan with only the water that still clings to them. Cook, covered, over a high heat, shaking the pan occasionally until the spinach is just wilted and still bright green. Drain. If using frozen spinach, cook it according to the packet instructions.

2 Bring at least 2 litres/3½ pints of water to the boil in a large saucepan. Add a pinch of salt. Cook the pasta for 8–12 minutes or according to packet instructions.

3 Meanwhile, heat the oil in a saucepan and fry the pine nuts until golden. Remove with a slotted spoon and drain on kitchen paper. Add the garlic to the oil in the pan and fry until golden. Add the anchovies, stir in the spinach and cook for
2–3 minutes or until heated through. Stir in the pine nuts and the sultanas, if using.

4 Drain the pasta, toss it in a little butter and turn into a warmed serving bowl. Top with the sauce and fork through roughly. Serve with plenty of Parmesan.

Fettuccine with Gorgonzola Sauce

Serves: **4**

Preparation time: 5 minutes

Cooking time: 8–12 minutes

500 g/1 lb fettuccine or other ribbon pasta
25 g/1 oz butter, plus extra to serve
250 g/8 oz Gorgonzola cheese, crumbled
150 ml/¼ pint double cream
2 tablespoons dry vermouth
1 teaspoon cornflour
2 tablespoons chopped sage
salt and pepper
sage leaves, to garnish

1 Bring at least 2 litres/3½ pints of water to the boil in a large saucepan. Add a pinch of salt. Cook the pasta for 8–12 minutes or according to packet instructions.

2 Meanwhile, melt the butter in a heavy-based saucepan. Sprinkle in the crumbled Gorgonzola and stir it over a very gentle heat for 2–3 minutes until the cheese is melted.

3 Pour in the cream, vermouth and cornflour, whisking well to amalgamate. Stir in the sage. Cook, whisking all the time, until the sauce boils and thickens. Taste the sauce and season with salt and pepper. Set aside.

4 Drain the pasta well and toss with a little butter. Reheat the sauce gently, whisking well. Pour it over the pasta and mix well. Serve immediately, garnished with sage leaves.

FOOD FACT • Gorgonzola is a creamy yellow semi-soft cheese, with characteristic blue-green veins and a rich, strong flavour. It was first produced over a thousand years ago in a village in the north of Italy called Gorgonzola, hence the name, and is one of the world's oldest cheeses. It can be eaten by itself or used in sauces, as here.

Pasta Arrabiata with Garlic Crumbs

This is a hot and spicy sauce with the added crunch of golden fried breadcrumbs, which are called mollica *or, more accurately,* mollica fritta. Mollica *is the Sicilian word for breadcrumbs. You can even toss plain pasta in the crumbs for a simple meal.*

Serves: **4–6**

Preparation time: 5 minutes

Cooking time: about 30 minutes

3 tablespoons olive oil
2 shallots, finely chopped
8 slices of unsmoked pancetta, chopped
2 teaspoons crushed chilli flakes
500 g/1 lb canned chopped tomatoes
500–750 g/1–1½ lb pasta shells
salt and pepper
parsley sprigs, to garnish
MOLLICA
6 slices of white bread, crusts removed
125 g/4 oz butter
2 garlic cloves, finely chopped

1 Heat the oil in a saucepan and fry the shallots and pancetta gently for 6–8 minutes until golden. Add the chilli flakes and chopped tomatoes, half cover the pan and simmer for 20 minutes until the sauce is thick and has reduced. Season to taste with salt and pepper.

2 Meanwhile, bring at least 2 litres/3½ pints of water to the boil in a large saucepan. Add a pinch of salt. Cook the pasta for 8–12 minutes or according to packet instructions.

3 To make the mollica, put the bread in a food processor and reduce to crumbs. Heat the butter in a frying pan, add the garlic and breadcrumbs and stir-fry until golden and crisp. (Don't let the crumbs catch and burn or the dish will be ruined.)

4 To serve, toss the cooked pasta with the tomato sauce and sprinkle each serving with some of the garlic crumbs. Garnish with parsley sprigs.

Spinach and Ricotta Ravioli

Serves: **4–6**

Preparation time: 45 minutes, plus resting

Cooking time: 3 minutes

PASTA
400 g/13 oz plain white flour
1 teaspoon salt
1 tablespoon olive oil
4 eggs, beaten
FILLING
500 g/1 lb frozen spinach, defrosted and
  squeezed dry
175 g/6 oz fresh ricotta or curd cheese
½ teaspoon freshly grated nutmeg
1 teaspoon salt
freshly ground black pepper
beaten egg, to seal
TO SERVE
125 g/4 oz butter, melted
25 g/1 oz freshly grated Parmesan cheese

1 To make the pasta, sift the flour and salt onto a clean work surface and make a well in the centre with your fist. Pour in the oil and beaten eggs and gradually mix into the flour with the fingers of one hand.

2 Knead the pasta until smooth, then wrap it in clingfilm and leave to rest for at least 30 minutes before attempting to roll it out. The pasta will be much more elastic after resting.

3 To make the filling, put the spinach and ricotta into a food processor with the nutmeg, salt and pepper to taste and process until smooth. Cover and refrigerate while you roll out the dough.

4 Cut the dough in half and wrap one half in clingfilm. Roll out the other half thinly to a rectangle on a lightly floured surface. Cover with a damp tea towel and repeat with the remaining dough.

5 Spoon or pipe small mounds of the filling in even rows on to one sheet of pasta, spacing them at 4 cm/1½ inch intervals. With a pastry brush, brush the spaces of dough between the mounds with beaten egg. Using a rolling pin, lift the remaining sheet of pasta over the sheet with the filling. Press down firmly between the mounds of filling, pushing out any pockets of trapped air.

6 Cut the pasta into squares with a serrated ravioli cutter or sharp knife, or cut it into semi-circles with an upturned glass. Transfer them to a floured tea towel and leave to rest for 1 hour before cooking.

7 Bring a large saucepan of salted water to the boil. Toss in the ravioli and cook for 3 minutes until puffy. Drain well and toss with melted butter. Serve immediately with freshly grated Parmesan.

Herb and Wild Mushroom Ravioli

These pretty, green, herb-speckled ravioli are filled with a mixture of wild mushrooms, with a hint of olive and sun-dried tomato to give an intense smoky flavour. They need no sauce other than a little melted butter and fresh Parmesan.

Serves: **4**

Preparation time: 45 minutes, plus resting

Cooking time: 5 minutes

PASTA

200 g/7 oz plain white flour

1 teaspoon salt

2 eggs

1 tablespoon olive oil

4 tablespoons chopped mixed tarragon, marjoram and parsley

FILLING

250 g/8 oz mixed wild mushrooms

50 g/2 oz butter or 2 tablespoons olive oil

2 shallots, finely chopped

25 g/1 oz Greek-style black olives, pitted and finely chopped

4 sun-dried tomato halves in oil, drained and finely chopped

1 tablespoon dry Marsala

freshly grated nutmeg

salt and pepper

beaten egg, to seal

TO FINISH

50 g/2 oz butter, melted

Parmesan shavings

a few sautéed wild mushrooms

herb sprigs

1 To make the pasta, sift the flour and salt onto a clean work surface and make a well in the centre with your fist.

2 Beat together the eggs and oil with a fork until thoroughly combined. Pour the beaten egg mixture into the well then sprinkle over the herbs.

3 Gradually mix the egg mixture and herbs into the flour with the fingers of one hand. Once the mixture looks lumpy and all the egg is mixed with the flour, bring the dough together with both hands and knead it into a rough ball shape. Scrape down and clean the work surface, then wash and dry your hands.

4 Knead the pasta for about 5–10 minutes until smooth and elastic. Wrap it in clingfilm or place it in a plastic bag and leave to rest at room temperature for at least 30 minutes before attempting to roll it out. The pasta will be much more elastic after resting.

5 To make the filling, carefully wipe or brush the mushrooms free from any dirt. (Try to avoid washing them as the flavour will be spoiled and the filling will get wet.) Chop them finely, stalks and all.

6 Melt the butter or oil, add the shallots and cook for about 5 minutes until soft and golden. Stir in the mushrooms, olives and sun-dried tomatoes and cook, stirring, over a high heat for about 2 minutes (no longer or the mushrooms will toughen). Sprinkle with the dry Marsala and cook for 1 minute longer. Season well with salt, pepper and grated nutmeg. Transfer to a bowl and leave to cool.

7 Unwrap the pasta and cut the dough in half. Wrap one half in clingfilm. Roll out the other half on a very lightly floured surface as thinly as possible to a 30 cm/12 inch square. Cover with a slightly damp tea towel and repeat with the remaining dough.

8 Place 16 heaped spoonfuls of filling on one sheet of pasta in 4 even rows, spacing them at 4 cm/1½ inch intervals. Using a pastry brush, brush the spaces of dough between the mounds with beaten egg. With a rolling pin, lift the remaining sheet of pasta over the dough with the filling. Press down firmly between the pockets of filling, pushing out any pockets of trapped air. Cut the pasta into squares with a serrated pastry cutter or a sharp knife. Transfer to a floured tea towel. (Do not make the ravioli too far in advance or the pasta will go grey.)

9 Bring a large saucepan of salted water to the boil, add a dash of olive oil and carefully add the ravioli. Bring back to the boil, turn off the heat and cover the pan with a tight-fitting lid. Leave for 5 minutes, then drain the ravioli well and return them to the pan and toss with the melted butter.

10 To serve, place 4 ravioli on each of 4 warmed plates. Shave some Parmesan over each portion and garnish with sautéed mushrooms and herb sprigs.

Gnocchi and Polenta

Potato Gnocchi

If made properly, these dumplings from northern Italy will be as light as a feather. The secret is to use floury potatoes, cook them in their skins, and mix the dough while still warm. A light hand is needed, and as little flour as possible. This recipe contains egg to make handling easier – the gnocchi will be a little firmer than those made without egg.

Serves: **4**

Preparation time: 30 minutes

Cooking time: 35 minutes

1 kg/2 lb floury potatoes, such as King
  Edward, unpeeled
50 g/2 oz butter
1 egg, beaten
250–300 g/8–10 oz plain white flour
semolina flour or plain flour, for sprinkling
salt
TO SERVE
melted butter
chopped sage
freshly grated Parmesan cheese

1 Cook the potatoes in boiling water for 20–30 minutes until very tender. Drain well. Alternatively, bake the potatoes in the oven until tender. Holding the potatoes in a tea towel, peel off the skins and pass the potatoes through a potato ricer or sieve into a bowl.

2 While the potatoes are still warm, add 1 teaspoon of salt, the butter, beaten egg and half of the flour. Lightly mix together, then turn out on to a floured board. Gradually, with a light hand, knead the rest of the flour into the dough until it is smooth, soft and a little sticky.

3 Roll the dough into long sausages, about 2.5 cm/1 inch thick and cut them into 1.5 cm/ ¾ inch pieces. Take each piece and roll it over the back of a fork with your floured thumb so the gnocchi form ridges on one side and an indentation on the other. Spread out the gnocchi on a tea towel sprinkled with semolina flour or plain white flour.

4 Bring a large pan of salted water to the boil. Drop in the gnocchi and cook for 2–3 minutes or until they float to the surface. Remove with a slotted spoon and toss with melted butter, chopped sage and plenty of grated Parmesan.

VARIATION • For a more elaborate dish, serve the potato gnocchi with the sauce of your choice. Both tomato-based sauces and creamy sauces taste delicious with gnocchi.

Lemon-scented Spinach and Ricotta Gnocchi

These are the lightest form of gnocchi, especially when they are made with the snowy white, fresh ricotta sold in Italian delicatessens. Fresh ricotta is made from the whey that is left after making cows' milk or sheep's milk cheese. The ricotta sold in tubs in supermarkets is made from pasteurized whole milk.

Serves: **4**

Preparation time: 30 minutes, plus standing and infusing

Cooking time: 20 minutes

625 g/1¼ lb fresh spinach, or 300 g/10 oz frozen spinach, defrosted
25 g/1 oz butter
1 shallot, finely chopped
finely grated rind of 1 lemon
150 g/5 oz fresh ricotta, sieved
75 g/3 oz plain white flour
2 egg yolks
75 g/3 oz freshly grated Parmesan cheese, plus extra to serve
freshly grated nutmeg
semolina flour or plain flour, for sprinkling
salt and pepper
herb sprigs, to garnish
SAUCE
2 lemons
175 g/6 oz unsalted butter
2 bay leaves

1 Remove the stalks from the fresh spinach and wash the leaves in several changes of cold water. Drain well and place in a large saucepan with just the water that clings to the leaves and cook until just wilted. Cool slightly, then squeeze out most of the moisture. Chop roughly and set aside. If using frozen spinach, squeeze out the moisture and roughly chop the spinach.

2 Melt the butter and fry the shallot until golden. Stir in the spinach and lemon rind, and cook for a couple of minutes until the spinach is coated and mixed with the butter and shallot. Tip into a large bowl.

3 Beat in the ricotta, flour, egg yolks and Parmesan. When they are thoroughly mixed, taste and season very well with salt, pepper and nutmeg. Cover and leave to stand for a couple of hours (or even overnight) in the refrigerator to firm up.

4 To make the sauce, scrub the lemons under hot water. Thinly pare the rind from both lemons with a potato peeler, avoiding the bitter white pith. Squeeze the juice from 1 lemon and reserve. Melt the butter in a small pan. Add the lemon rind and bay leaves and heat gently for 2 minutes then remove the pan from the heat and leave the sauce in a warm place to infuse for at least 1 hour (the longer this can be left the better).

5 Take large teaspoonfuls of the gnocchi mixture and quickly roll them into small cork shapes. Place on a tray lined with a tea towel sprinkled with semolina flour or plain flour.

6 Reheat the butter and strain it into a clean pan. Stir in the lemon juice and bring to the boil (it will splutter) and season with salt and pepper. Keep warm. Spoon a third of this sauce into a warmed shallow serving dish.

7 Bring a large pan of salted water to the boil, drop in all the gnocchi at once and cook them for 2–3 minutes after the water returns to the boil. Lift out with a slotted spoon, drain well and transfer to the warmed dish. Pour over the lemony butter and serve with some freshly grated Parmesan, garnished with herb sprigs.

Baked Gnocchi with Smoked Pancetta, Parmesan and Sage

These gnocchi are made from semolina, cheese, milk and sage. When the mixture is cold, it is cut into shapes, layered in a baking dish with butter and baked until golden. This is a marvellous dish served with a fresh tomato sauce, or with game.

Serves: **4**

Preparation time: 15 minutes, plus cooling

Cooking time: 25–30 minutes

Oven temperature: 230°C/450°F/Gas Mark 8

FOOD FACT • Gnocchi are fun to prepare. They can be made either from potato or, as in this recipe, from semolina.

1 litre/1¾ pints milk
250 g/8 oz semolina
175 g/6 oz freshly grated Parmesan cheese
125 g/4 oz butter
2 egg yolks
1 tablespoon Dijon mustard
2 tablespoons chopped sage
3 tablespoons chopped parsley
150 g/5 oz rolled unsmoked pancetta, thinly sliced
handful of sage leaves
salt and pepper

1 Pour the milk into a saucepan and whisk in the semolina. Bring slowly to the boil, stirring all the time until it really thickens – this takes about 10 minutes.

2 Beat in half of the Parmesan, half of the butter, the egg yolks, mustard, chopped sage and parsley. Taste and season well with salt and pepper. Line a baking sheet with clingfilm and spread the mixture over it to a depth of 1 cm/½ inch. Leave for about 2 hours to cool and set.

3 When the gnocchi has set, cut it into triangles or circles with a 3.5 cm/1½ inch biscuit cutter.

4 Butter an ovenproof dish well and scatter the gnocchi trimmings over the base. Dot with half of the remaining butter, scatter over half of the pancetta and sprinkle with a little of the remaining Parmesan. Arrange the gnocchi shapes in a single layer over the trimmings. Dot with the rest of the butter and scatter over the remaining pancetta and the sage leaves.

5 Sprinkle with the remaining Parmesan and bake in a preheated oven, 230°C/450°F/Gas Mark 8, for 15–20 minutes until the gnocchi are golden and crusty and the bacon crisp. Leave to stand for 5 minutes before serving.

Deep-fried Gnocchi with Salsa Rossa

The secret of this sauce from Piedmont lies in its long, slow cooking. The sauce is rich and concentrated, and slightly sweet and sour – perfect for dipping these crisp deep-fried snacks with their soft cheesy centres.

Serves: **6 as a snack**

Preparation time: 25 minutes, plus chilling

Cooking time: 2–3 hours

SALSA ROSSA
7 very ripe tomatoes, chopped
1 carrot, finely chopped
2 onions, finely chopped
3 garlic cloves, finely chopped
1 small dried red chilli, deseeded
3 tablespoons granulated sugar
1 tablespoon red wine vinegar
about 1 tablespoon olive oil
salt and pepper
GNOCCHI
500 ml/17 fl oz milk
250 g/8 oz semolina
75 g/3 oz freshly grated Parmesan cheese
50 g/2 oz butter
1 egg yolk
pinch of chilli powder
freshly grated nutmeg
plain flour, for coating
2 eggs, beaten
dry breadcrumbs, for coating
salt and pepper
oil, for deep-frying

1 To make the sauce, put the tomatoes, carrot, onions, garlic, chilli, sugar and vinegar into a heavy saucepan with the olive oil. Bring to the boil, then turn down the heat, cover the pan and simmer for 2–3 hours until the sauce is very soft.

2 To make the gnocchi, pour the milk into a saucepan and whisk in the semolina. Bring the mixture slowly to the boil, stirring all the time until it really thickens – about 10 minutes.

3 Beat in the Parmesan, butter, egg yolk, chilli and plenty of nutmeg. Taste and season well with salt and pepper. Line a baking sheet or Swiss roll tin with clingfilm and spread out the mixture to a depth of 1 cm/½ inch. Leave to cool then chill in the refrigerator for about 2 hours.

4 When the sauce is ready, remove and discard the chilli and blend the sauce in a liquidizer or pass through a fine sieve. Taste and season with salt and pepper and a little extra olive oil. Reheat the salsa rossa to serve with the gnocchi.

5 When the gnocchi is well-chilled and set, cut it into bite-sized triangles with a wet knife. Dip each triangle in flour, then beaten egg and finally in the breadcrumbs. Heat the oil to 180°C/350°F or until a cube of bread browns in 30 seconds, then deep-fry the gnocchi in batches for about 2–3 minutes until golden and crisp. Sprinkle with salt. Allow to cool slightly then serve with the salsa rossa.

Oven-baked Polenta

This is an amazingly easy way to cook real polenta without stirring it for hours. Serve with moist meat or vegetable dishes, or dress with garlic butter, rosemary sprigs and grated Parmesan.

Serves: **6–8**

Cooking time: 1 hour 15 minutes

Oven temperature: 190°C/375°F/Gas Mark 5

15–25 g/½–1 oz butter
1.8 litres/3 pints water
2 teaspoons salt
375 g/12 oz polenta flour (not instant)
TO SERVE
garlic butter
rosemary sprigs
grated Parmesan cheese

1 Butter a large ovenproof dish.

2 Pour the water into a large saucepan, add the salt and bring to the boil. Remove the pan from the heat and sprinkle the polenta into the water in a continuous shower, stirring or whisking to prevent lumps forming. Return the pan to the heat, bring to the boil then simmer for 5 minutes, stirring constantly.

3 Spoon the polenta into the prepared dish, levelling the top. Cover with buttered or oiled kitchen foil and cook in a preheated oven, 190°C/375°F/Gas Mark 5, for 1 hour. Remove the dish from the oven, loosen the polenta and turn it out on to a board. Slice with a sharp knife and serve topped with garlic butter, rosemary sprigs and Parmesan, or as an accompaniment to a meat or vegetable dish.

FOOD FACT • Polenta can be frozen quite successfully for up to 3 months. Be sure to let it defrost thoroughly before cooking.

Polenta Chips

Not strictly Italian but very good all the same, these polenta chips can be served instead of roast potatoes or potato chips. They are a pale golden colour, crisp on the outside and soft on the inside.

Serves: **4**

Preparation time: 35 minutes, plus chilling

Cooking time: 25–30 minutes

50 g/2 oz butter
600 ml/1 pint water
1 teaspoon salt
125 g/4 oz polenta flour
plain white flour, for rolling
salt and paprika pepper
oil, for deep-frying

1 Put the butter and water into a saucepan with the salt and bring to the boil. Remove the pan from the heat and pour in the polenta, whisking all the time to prevent lumps forming. Return the pan to the heat and cook, stirring constantly, for 15 minutes or until the mixture leaves the sides of the pan. Turn the polenta out into a shallow oiled dish, smooth the top and leave to cool. Cover and chill until firm.

2 Turn out the firm polenta onto wet greaseproof paper and cut it into thick chips with a wet knife.

3 Heat the oil to 180°C/350°F or until a cube of bread browns in 30 seconds. Roll the chips in a little flour and deep-fry in batches for 6–8 minutes until pale golden brown and crisp. Drain on absorbent kitchen paper and sprinkle with salt and paprika. Keep warm in a low oven with the door ajar until needed.

Soft Rosemary and Garlic Polenta

Serve this polenta dish as an alternative to mashed potatoes with rich stews, game dishes and ragùs. It should be served as soon as it is ready, as it has a tendency to thicken if it is left to stand. This recipe uses quick-cook polenta for convenience.

Serves: **4**

Preparation time: 10 minutes

Cooking time: 15 minutes

1.5 litres/2½ pints cold water
125 g/4 oz butter
4 large garlic cloves, finely chopped
3 tablespoons chopped rosemary
300 g/10 oz instant or quick-cook polenta
salt and pepper
rosemary sprigs, to garnish

1 Bring the water to the boil in a large saucepan with 2 teaspoons of salt.

2 Melt half the butter and fry the garlic until golden. Stir in the rosemary and set aside.

3 Sprinkle the polenta into the boiling water in a continuous shower, stirring or whisking all the time to prevent lumps forming. Beat in the garlic and rosemary then simmer for 5–10 minutes, stirring constantly until the polenta has thickened like soft mashed potato. Season well with salt and pepper, beat in the remaining butter and serve immediately, garnished with rosemary sprigs.

FOOD FACT • Rosemary is a favourite Italian herb. It has a powerful flavour, and should therefore be used with caution if it is not to be too dominant.

Fish and Seafood

Whole Fish Baked in a Salt Crust

Don't be tempted to scale and gut the fish – the scales protect it from the salt and, if gutted, the fish would lose a lot of moisture. The beauty of this dish lies in its simplicity.

Serves: **8**

Preparation time: 15 minutes

Cooking time: 1 hour

Oven temperature: 190°C/375°F/Gas Mark 5

oil, for greasing
2 egg whites
6 tablespoons water
about 2 kg/4 lb sea salt, depending on size of the dishes
2 x 2 kg/4 lb whole fish, unscaled and ungutted
large handful of dill or wild fennel fronds

1 Choose 2 oval or rectangular baking dishes into which the fish will fit very comfortably without touching the edges. Lightly brush the dishes with oil.

2 Lightly beat the egg whites with the water and then mix with the sea salt – do this with your hands, like rubbing in the fat when making pastry.

3 Cover the bottom of each dish with a 2.5 cm/1 inch layer of sea salt. Put the fish on the salt, cover with dill fronds, top with a thick layer of the remaining moist salt and bake in a preheated oven, 190°C/375°F/Gas Mark 5, for about 1 hour.

4 Remove the dishes from the oven and leave to rest for 10 minutes. Carry them ceremoniously to the table and crack the crust open – you may need a hammer for this! The herbs and skin should come away with the salt crust. Serve the fish as quickly as possible.

VARIATION • Whole sea trout, salmon and sea bass, even red snapper, all work well treated this way – the flavour is intense but not at all salty, and the flesh is moist.

Roast Garlic-studded Monkfish

Firm-fleshed monkfish, studded with garlic and scented with bay, is kept moist by roasting over a bed of juicy vegetables.

Serves: **4**

Preparation time: 20 minutes, plus marinating

Cooking time: 20 minutes

Oven temperature: 220°C/425°F/Gas Mark 7

1 kg/2 lb monkfish tail
3–4 bay leaves
1 teaspoon fennel seeds
4–6 garlic cloves, cut into thick slivers
4 tablespoons olive oil
a few thyme sprigs
2 red peppers, halved, deseeded and roughly chopped
1 aubergine, cut into bite-sized chunks
2 courgettes, cut into bite-sized chunks
3 ripe plum tomatoes, cut into chunks
3 tablespoons lemon juice
salt and pepper
TO GARNISH
2 tablespoons salted capers, rinsed and chopped
3 tablespoons chopped parsley

1 Trim any membrane and dark meat from the monkfish. Remove the central bone by slitting the fish down the middle until you reach the bone. Turn the fish over and do the same on the other side. Ease out the bone, gently scraping the flesh away with the tip of a knife.

2 Lay the bay leaves over the inside of one fillet, and scatter over the fennel seeds. Lay the other fillet on top and tie up at 2.5 cm/ 1 inch intervals with fine string. The fish should look like a long pork fillet.

3 With the tip of a sharp knife, make slits all over the monkfish and push in the garlic slivers. Pour the olive oil, thyme and a little ground black pepper into a glass dish and add the monkfish, turning well to coat. Cover and leave to marinate in the refrigerator for at least 2 hours or, better still, overnight.

4 Remove the fish from the marinade. Pour 2 tablespoons of the marinade into a heavy nonstick frying pan and heat until almost smoking. Add the monkfish and turn to seal for 2–3 minutes. Remove the fish and set aside.

5 In the same pan, heat the remaining marinade and quickly brown the peppers, aubergine and courgettes. Transfer the vegetables to a heavy shallow baking dish, set the monkfish on top and add the tomatoes and lemon juice. Bake in a preheated oven, 220°C/425°F/Gas Mark 7, for 20 minutes, basting occasionally and turning the vegetables from time to time.

6 Take the monkfish out of the oven and remove the string. Cut the fish into thick slices, discarding the bay leaves. Season the vegetables with salt and pepper to taste. Serve the monkfish on the roasted vegetable stew, garnished with chopped capers and parsley.

Braised Sea Bass with Fennel and Green Olives

Serves: **4**

Preparation time: 15 minutes

Cooking time: 35 minutes

Oven temperature: 220°C/425°F/Gas Mark 7

1.25 kg/2½ lb sea bass, scaled and gutted
few rosemary sprigs
2 large fennel bulbs
150 ml/¼ pint good olive oil
4 tablespoons lemon juice
1 tablespoon dried oregano
3 tablespoons chopped parsley
8 large green olives, pitted
150 ml/¼ pint dry white wine
salt and pepper
fennel fronds, to garnish

1 Wash the fish inside and out. Fill the cavity with sprigs of rosemary.

2 Cut the fennel bulbs in half lengthways, cut out the core and slice thickly. Blanch in boiling salted water for 5 minutes. Drain.

3 Whisk together the oil, lemon juice, oregano, parsley and salt and pepper in a bowl and stir in the fennel to coat. Tip this mixture into a shallow, oval ovenproof dish that will take the fish as well. Lay the fish on top of the fennel and pour over any remaining liquid. Tuck in the olives and pour over the wine.

4 Bake in a preheated oven, 220°C/425°F/Gas Mark 7, for 30 minutes. Open the oven and spoon the juices over the fish and stir the fennel around. Turn off the oven leaving the fish to set for 5 minutes before serving immediately, garnished with fennel fronds.

VARIATION • Sea bream may also be used in this recipe.

Blue-cooked Trout

This is a recipe from the cold rivers and streams in the mountains. The fish is so fresh it needs no adulteration with sauces – just a few buttered new potatoes.

Serves: **4**

Preparation time: 10 minutes

Cooking time: 30–40 minutes

4 very fresh trout, still coated with slime if
   possible, gutted through the gills
4 tablespoons white wine vinegar
lemon wedges, to serve
COURT BOUILLON
1 onion, thinly sliced
1 carrot, thinly sliced
1 celery stick, thinly sliced
2 parsley sprigs
2 thyme sprigs
1 bay leaf
4 peppercorns, crushed
75 ml/3 fl oz white wine vinegar
1.5 litres/2½ pints water
salt

1 Lay the trout in a dish and sprinkle with the vinegar. Cover and chill while preparing the court bouillon.

2 To make the court bouillon, put the onion, carrot, celery, parsley, thyme, bay leaf, peppercorns, vinegar and water into a saucepan with a pinch of salt. Bring to the boil, then turn down the heat, cover the pan and simmer for 30 minutes. Strain the court bouillon and return it to the pan. Heat to barely simmering.

3 Drop the trout into the hot liquid. Remove the pan from the heat and leave the fish to cook for 7–8 minutes. They will turn grey-blue and curl up slightly. Lift them out of the pan as soon as they are done and arrange them on a warmed platter with the lemon wedges.

Wine

Italy has been making wine for some 2,500 years, ever since the Roman legions took vines to every outpost of the Empire, becoming, as a result, largely responsible for the spread of wine-making throughout western Europe. Wine is a way of life on this large peninsula, where bread, wine and olive oil have been the dietary holy trinity for centuries.

Italy is now the largest wine producer in the world, accounting for almost a quarter of the world's entire output. Although vast amounts of wine are consumed in Italy itself, with some 120 bottles being drunk per person per year, there are also increasing amounts of wine being exported all around the world, and you will not therefore be in the least surprised to find a large selection of good Italian wines on the shelves of your local off-licence or your nearest supermarket.

Italian wines are easily distinguishable from the wines of other countries because a large majority of them are made from indigenous varieties of hill-grown grapes. The most well known of these include the Trebbiano, Frascati and Orvieto varieties. Italian wines also differ markedly from each other, their individual characteristics being dependent upon a number of factors, including the soil, climate, variety of grape and particular method of vinification used.

As long ago as in 1963, Italy passed a law giving nationally enforceable protection to named wines from specific areas. It created the Denominazione di Origine Controllata (D.O.C.), which is the Italian equivalent of the French Appellation d'Origine Contrôlée. It means that only wines that have been produced within a legally delimited area can be sold under the name of that area. The letters D.O.C. on the label also mean that the wine is of particular reputation and worth. In addition to this, there is also a special rare denomination, D.O.C.G. – not merely controlled (C) but guaranteed (G) – which denotes really outstanding wines. Recently, yet another category was created for wines of lesser worth, the Indicazione Geografica Tipica (IGT), which is an equivalent of Vin de Pays in France or Landwein in neighbouring Germany.

The problem with these regulations is that they are rather complicated. As a result of this, they don't, in the end, tell customers very much. Compare this system with France, for example, which has a clear geographical system of appellations, or with the easily understandable Californian varietal system. In both these cases, you know exactly what you are paying for – in France it is a wine produced in a narrowly defined geographical area, and in California it is a particular style of wine that is made from a particular grape.

In Italy, though, you don't necessarily know exactly what you are purchasing because they have, in certain cases, given a geographical name to wines made with the same grapes outside the original appellation. Chianti, for instance, is made in large parts of Tuscany, between Florence and Siena, well away from the original area around Castellina where Chianti Classico was first made.

Regional differences

Every region of Italy makes its own local wine, from the Italian Alps in the north to the Mediterranean islands, which are closer to north Africa than to the Italian mainland. So, wherever you are in Italy, there will always be a large selection of local wines to choose from and these are often remarkably good. In fact, when you are travelling around Italy, it is often better, at least in terms of value for money, to drink the wine of your particular locality, as in many cases a carafe of unnamed house wine may well turn out to be surprisingly good.

Piemonte, for example (which literally means 'the foot of the mountain' in Italian), produces the dramatic reds Barolo, Barbera, a robust everyday wine which is grown throughout the region, and Barbaresco, as well as the popular semi-sweet sparkling Asti Spumante; Veneto, which produces more wine than any other region – apart from Sicily and Apulia, which is the true heel of Italy – produces Valpolicella, Soave, the popular fresh white, and Bardolino; Emilia-Romagna produces Lambrusco, the frothy, fruity red, white and rosé designed to be drunk young; Lazio – whose capital is Rome – produces Frascati, which is the most famous and most important of the wines made in the volcanic hills south-east of Rome; Umbria produces Orvieto, which is a popular and clean-tasting white; and from the beautiful hills and valleys of Tuscany comes the wonderful Chianti Classico, which is probably Italy's best-known wine.

There is so much local wine available throughout Italy that it is not only drunk but also often used as an important ingredient in many local dishes, where it helps to both add flavour and tenderise the meat. Dry whites and reds are used in meat and poultry dishes, such as Beef Braised in Barolo (see page 168), fish stews and soups, for example Sicilian Fish Soup (see page 28) and also in risottos, such as Red Wine Risotto (see page 70), where they add a richness of flavour. Marsala, the rich fortified Sicilian wine, is used in many Italian sweet dishes, as well as in chicken, veal, duck and ham recipes.

Which wine with which food?

The lighter Italian red wines, such as Valpolicella, are ideal partners for the majority of pasta and pizza dishes. Try them, too, with roast meats.

The big robust reds, such as Barolo, Barbaresco and Gattinara, are excellent with rich meaty stews, game recipes, risottos and cheese dishes.

Barbera, a red from Piemonte, goes particularly well with Parma ham from the neighbouring region of Emilia-Romagna.

Chianti and Valpolicella are well suited to the traditional hearty soups from the north of Italy, such as La Ribollita or Tuscan Bean and Vegetable Soup (see page 26). Chianti is also good with pasta and grills.

The white wines from Veneto, including Pinot Grigio and Soave, are perfect accompaniments for the region's many fish dishes. Pinot Grigio also goes well with figs and especially well with asparagus, which is worth remembering because there are not many wines that do.

In the summer, when you are dining al fresco or eating salads, try the soft golden tasting Frascati, and with sweet desserts, sweet Asti Spumante is perfect. Vin Santo, a sweet yet strong, barrel–aged wine from Tuscany, is ideal for dipping your biscotti into.

Fortified wines

Fortified wines are stronger than table wines but are excellent for use in cooking.

Marsala, for example, which is a rich fortified Sicilian wine, is often used for flavouring all sorts of dishes, both sweet and savoury, for example Veal and Sage Escalopes (see page 174). It can be sweet or dry. The dry version is drunk as an apéritif and the sweet as a dessert wine. A medium Marsala is the best choice for cooking and it will keep for months once the bottle has been opened.

Dry white vermouth is another excellent wine to use for cooking, and imparts a good flavour to many savoury recipes. Again, it will keep well after opening.

Red Mullet 'in Cartoccio'

Serves: **4**

Preparation time: 25 minutes

Cooking time: 20 minutes

Oven temperature: 190°C/375°F/Gas Mark 5

2 oranges, preferably tarrocchi or blood oranges
2 tablespoons olive oil, plus extra for brushing
8 bay leaves
4 x 250 g/8 oz red mullet, cleaned and scaled
salt and pepper

1 Cut 4 rectangles of baking parchment or greaseproof paper big enough to loosely wrap a fish. Brush the rectangles with a little oil.

2 Grate the rind from the oranges, mix with the olive oil, season with salt and pepper and set aside. Peel the oranges as you would an apple, removing all the white pith. Slice them thinly. Place a bay leaf in the cavity of each fish and one on top.

3 Use half of the orange slices to make a row to one side of each parchment rectangle. Put the fish on the slices and cover them with the remaining orange slices. Drizzle with the oil and rind. Season well.

4 Fold the free paper loosely over the fish and twist the edges together to seal. Lift the packages on to a baking sheet and bake in a preheated oven, 190°C/375°F/Gas Mark 5, for 20 minutes. Serve immediately, opening the packages at the table.

Red Mullet with Mint Sauce

This is an ancient Arab recipe, which is still used in Palermo today. Red mullet can be served slightly underdone – they will take about 1–3 minutes on each side, depending on the size of the fish.

Serves: **6**

Preparation time: 10 minutes

Cooking time: 2–6 minutes

50 g/2 oz stale breadcrumbs
3 tablespoons white wine vinegar
3 tablespoons chopped mint
3 tablespoons chopped parsley
1 tablespoon salted capers, rinsed
1 egg, beaten
2 teaspoons sugar
2 teaspoons anchovy paste or 2 anchovy fillets, drained
150 ml/¼ pint fruity olive oil, plus extra for frying
1 kg/2 lb small red mullet, cleaned and scaled
flour, for coating
salt and pepper
TO GARNISH
lemon wedges
mint sprigs

1 Moisten the breadcrumbs with 2 tablespoons of the vinegar and a little water. Let the breadcrumbs stand for a couple of minutes then squeeze out the moisture.

2 Put the breadcrumbs into a food processor and add the mint, parsley, capers, egg, sugar and anchovy paste. Blend until smooth. With the machine running, gradually add the oil in a steady stream as if you were making mayonnaise. Taste and season with salt and pepper then add the remaining vinegar if necessary. The sauce should be pale green and slightly sweet and sour. Transfer to a bowl.

3 Lightly coat the fish in seasoned flour and fry for 1–3 minutes on each side until golden. Arrange the fish on a warmed platter garnished with lemon wedges and mint sprigs and serve the sauce separately.

Tuna Steaks Glazed with Balsamic Vinegar and Basil Oil

This is a modern version of a dish that is described as agrodolce, *or sweet and sour. The use of soy sauce is not strictly Italian.*

Serves: **4**

Preparation time: 10 minutes, plus marinating

Cooking time: 8 minutes

4 x 175 g/6 oz tuna steaks, with the skin left on
2 tablespoons balsamic vinegar
2 teaspoons soy sauce
75 ml/3 fl oz extra virgin olive oil
50 g/2 oz basil leaves, plus extra to garnish
salt and pepper

1 Place the tuna steaks in a shallow non-corrosive dish. Mix together the balsamic vinegar and soy sauce and pour over the tuna steaks, turning them so they are thoroughly coated. Cover the dish and leave to marinate in the refrigerator for at least 30 minutes.

2 Pour the olive oil into a blender or food processor, add the basil and liquidize until smooth. Season with salt and pepper, pour into a bowl, cover and leave to infuse.

3 Preheat a grill or barbecue. Remove the tuna from the marinade and place on a foil-lined grill pan. Grill the steaks for about 4 minutes on each side, brushing with the marinade.

4 Whisk the basil oil again then drizzle it over the steaks, to serve. Garnish with basil leaves.

FOOD FACT • Balsamic vinegar is the king of vinegars and lends a deliciously sweet flavour to this dish.

Baked Swordfish Rolls

These swordfish rolls are delicious served with Sardines to Look Like Fig-Peckers (see page 150).

Serves: **4**

Preparation time: 25 minutes, plus chilling

Cooking time: 12 minutes

8 x 5 mm/¼ inch slices of swordfish, total weight 750 g/1½ lb
1 garlic clove, crushed
1 tablespoon chopped sage
2 dried bay leaves, crumbled
1 tablespoon chopped rosemary
1 teaspoon dried chilli flakes
1 mozzarella, weighing about 150 g/5 oz, drained and grated
6 slices of bread, crusts removed, made into breadcrumbs
2 tablespoons freshly grated Pecorino or Parmesan cheese
1 teaspoon dried oregano
2 eggs, beaten
fresh bay leaves
2 lemons, cut into wedges
4 small red onions, cut into wedges
olive oil, for drizzling
salt and pepper

1 Soak some bamboo skewers in cold water for at least 20 minutes.

2 Put the slices of swordfish between sheets of clingfilm and flatten them with a wooden mallet until they are very thin, but do not tear the flesh.

3 Mix the garlic with the sage, crumbled bay leaves, rosemary, chilli flakes and mozzarella. Spread this mixture evenly over the swordfish slices and season them with salt and pepper.

4 Roll up each slice tightly and secure with a cocktail stick if necessary. Coat the rolls in a little olive oil then chill for at least 1 hour to firm up.

5 Mix the breadcrumbs with the Pecorino or Parmesan and oregano. Dip each roll into the beaten egg, then the breadcrumb mixture to coat. Thread the rolls on to double bamboo skewers alternating them with the bay leaves, lemon wedges and onion wedges.

6 Drizzle the skewers with a little olive oil and grill or barbecue for 6 minutes on each side.

FOOD FACT • Mozzarella is a white curd cheese with a soft chewy texture and a mild milky flavour. It is moulded into balls and wrapped in small bags with whey added to keep the cheese moist. It can be eaten fresh in salads, or it can be cooked as it has good melting qualities.

Monkfish in Salsa d'Agrumi

Agrumi is a collective term for all citrus fruits, which seem to marry very well with fish.

Serves: **4**

Preparation time: 20 minutes

Cooking time: 10 minutes

875 g/1¾ lb monkfish
flour, for coating
2 tablespoons olive oil
finely grated rind and juice of 1 lemon
finely grated rind and juice of 1 orange
150 ml/¼ pint dry white wine
2 tablespoons chopped parsley
salt and pepper
TO GARNISH
orange rind
parsley sprigs
orange and lemon wedges

VARIATION • This citrus salsa is also particularly good with sole rather than monkfish.

1 Trim any membrane and dark meat from the monkfish. Remove the central bone by slitting the fish down the middle until you reach the bone. Turn the fish over and do the same on the other side. Ease out the bone, by gently scraping the flesh away with the tip of a knife. Cut the fish into large chunks and then toss them in seasoned flour, shaking off the excess.

2 Heat the oil in a nonstick frying pan and fry the fish until golden all over. Remove the fish to a plate.

3 Add the lemon and orange rind and juice to the pan with the wine and boil rapidly to evaporate the alcohol. Turn down the heat, return the fish to the pan and simmer gently for 3–4 minutes or until the fish is cooked. Stir in the parsley and salt and pepper to taste. Lift out the fish on to a warmed serving dish. Boil the sauce to reduce it a little more then pour it over the fish. Serve immediately garnished with orange rind, parsley sprigs and orange and lemon wedges.

Grilled Swordfish with Toasted Almond and Parsley Pesto

Serve this herb and nut pesto with any grilled, poached or baked fish.

Serves: **4**

Preparation time: 10 minutes

Cooking time: 10 minutes

125 g/4 oz unblanched whole almonds
1 garlic clove, crushed
2 tablespoons freshly grated Parmesan cheese
50 g/2 oz parsley, roughly chopped
200 ml/7 fl oz extra virgin olive oil
2 tablespoons fresh ricotta cheese
4 x 175 g/6 oz swordfish steaks
olive oil, for brushing
salt and pepper
lemon wedges, to garnish

1 Spread the almonds on a baking sheet and place it under a preheated grill for 2–3 minutes, turning the almonds often until they are toasted and golden. (You may have to break one open to see.)

2 Place half of the toasted almonds in a blender or food processor with the garlic, Parmesan, parsley, olive oil, ricotta and salt and pepper and blend until smooth, scraping down the sides of the bowl if necessary. Roughly chop the remaining almonds and stir into the pesto.

3 Brush the swordfish steaks with olive oil and grill under a preheated hot grill for 2–3 minutes on each side or until just cooked through. Season with salt and pepper and serve the fish with the pesto, garnished with lemon wedges.

FOOD FACT • Pesto is a classic Italian sauce, usually made from pine nuts and basil. Here, for a change, it is made from almonds and parsley.

Sardines to Look Like Fig-Peckers

This dish gets its name because the sardines are said to look like fig-peckers, which are little birds, when assembled in their dish. Typical Sicilian ingredients are used here – orange rind and juice, pine nuts, capers and currants. It is usually served as a light lunch dish, or with other fish dishes as a main course.

Serves: **4**

Preparation time: 25 minutes

Cooking time: 10 minutes

Oven temperature: 200°C/400°F/Gas Mark 6

16 fresh sardines
50 g/2 oz pine nuts, toasted
50 g/2 oz currants
3 tablespoons chopped parsley
1 tablespoon salted capers, rinsed and chopped
finely grated rind and juice of 1 orange
a few bay leaves
150 ml/¼ pint good olive oil
salt and pepper

1 Scale the sardines, cut off the heads and slit open the bellies. Remove the guts under running water. Slide your thumb along the backbone to release the flesh along its length. Take hold of the backbone at the head end and lift it out. The fish should now be open like a book.

2 Mix together the pine nuts, currants, parsley, capers, orange rind and salt and pepper. Place a spoonful of the mixture on the flesh-side of each fish. Roll up the sardines from the head end and secure them with a cocktail stick if necessary.

3 Place the rolled sardines, tightly packed together in rows with their tails sticking upwards, in a dish in which they will fit snugly. Tuck a few bay leaves in between them. Whisk together the orange juice and olive oil and pour it over the fish. Season the fish well and bake in a preheated oven, 200°C/400°F/Gas Mark 6, for 10 minutes. Remove from the oven and leave to cool. Serve at room temperature.

Salmoriglio Sauce for Grilled Fish

All the scents of the south are here when you spoon the dressing over the hot fish. Dried oregano is preferred to fresh in this dish as it has a more concentrated flavour and is not as bitter. This sauce is beloved by the Sicilians who serve it on all charcoal grilled and barbecued fish and seafood, including squid and prawns.

Serves: **4**

Preparation time: 10 minutes

175 ml/6 fl oz extra virgin olive oil
5 tablespoons lemon juice
2 teaspoons dried oregano
2 garlic cloves, finely chopped
2 tablespoons chopped parsley

1 Whisk all the ingredients together until thick. Lay the grilled fish or seafood on a platter. Spoon the sauce over at the last moment.

FOOD FACT • Oregano is wild marjoram and is slightly stronger and spicier than its relative. It is highly prized by the Italians and is often used in pizzas and sauces.

Lobster Sauce with Spaghetti

This sauce is made from the tiny sweet lobsters found on the south-west coast of Sicily.

Serves: **6**

Preparation time: 10 minutes

Cooking time: 25 minutes

3 small live lobsters or lobster tails, weighing
  about 400 g/13 oz each
750 g/1½ lb dried spaghetti
3 tablespoons olive oil
2–3 garlic cloves, chopped
large pinch of crushed dried chilli
1 glass dry white wine
1 tablespoon chopped parsley, plus extra to
  garnish
salt and pepper

1 Bring a large pan of salted water to the boil, drop in 1 lobster and simmer for 12 minutes. Leave to cool, then remove the flesh from the shells.

2 Bring at least 2 litres/3½ pints water to the boil in a large saucepan. Add a pinch of salt. Cook the pasta for 8–12 minutes or according to packet instructions.

3 While the spaghetti is cooking, split the other 2 lobsters in half lengthways, remove and discard the stomach sacs, then chop them into large pieces, legs, head and all.

4 Heat the oil in a sauté pan, add the garlic, chilli and chopped lobster. Sauté for a couple of minutes, then add the wine. Bring to the boil, then add the boiled lobster meat and stir in the parsley. Season to taste with salt and pepper.

5 Toss the lobster with the freshly cooked spaghetti, garnish with parsley and eat it from the shells with your fingers – sucking the shells is part of the fun.

VARIATION • If you cannot find any small lobsters, the equivalent weight in Dublin Bay prawns will do just as well.

Jumping Squid with Sweet and Sour Chilli and Aubergine

This recipe acquired its unusual name because the squid tend to jump around when they are cooked in a really hot griddle pan.

Serves: **4**

Preparation time: 20 minutes, plus marinating

Cooking time: 15 minutes

750 g/1½ lb baby squid
2 small red chillies, deseeded and chopped
2 garlic cloves
1 tablespoon sugar
finely grated rind and juice of 1 lemon
4 tablespoons olive oil
vegetable oil, for deep-frying
2 aubergines, very thinly sliced
salt and pepper
lemon wedges, to serve

1 To clean a squid, pull the head from the body and remove the transparent 'pen' from the inside. Pull off the skin, rinse the body and slice it into rings. Trim the tentacles by holding the head just below the eyes and cutting the tentacles away. Rinse, discarding the head and the entrails.

2 Place the chillies, garlic, sugar, lemon rind and juice and olive oil in a food processor or blender and liquidize until smooth. Transfer to a bowl.

3 Stir the squid rings and tentacles into the marinade, cover and leave to marinate for 2 hours.

4 While the squid are marinating, heat the oil in a large saucepan. Deep-fry the aubergine slices in the oil in batches until brown and crisp. Spread out on kitchen paper to drain, then transfer to a warmed serving dish. Put to one side and keep warm.

5 Remove the squid from the marinade, reserving the marinade.

6 Heat a heavy frying pan until smoking and brush with oil. Sauté the squid for 1–2 minutes, tossing them all the time until caramelized. (The pan must be very hot.) Spoon the squid over the warm fried aubergine. Pour the marinade into the pan and heat it gently, then pour it over the squid. Serve immediately with lemon wedges.

Mussels alla Marinara

Serves: **4**

Preparation time: 15 minutes

Cooking time: 10 minutes

2 kg/4 lb fresh mussels
3 tablespoons olive oil
4 garlic cloves, chopped
150 ml/¼ pint dry white wine
400 g/13 oz can chopped tomatoes
1 small fresh red chilli, deseeded and finely
  chopped
4 tablespoons chopped parsley
salt and pepper
crusty bread, to serve

1 Scrub the mussels and remove the beards. Wash them in several changes of water and discard any that are not firmly closed.

2 Heat the oil in a large saucepan and fry the garlic until golden. Add the wine, tomatoes, chilli and half of the parsley and bring to the boil. Season well with salt and pepper, add the mussels and cover the pan. Cook over a brisk heat, shaking the pan, until all the mussels are open. Stir well. Discard any mussels that have not opened.

3 To serve, scatter the remaining parsley over the mussels and serve with crusty bread.

Mixed Deep-fried Seafood

All types of seafood can be coated with this light batter known as pastella. *This dish is quick to make and best eaten with the fingers!*

Serves: **4–6**

Preparation time: 20 minutes

Cooking time: 15 minutes

175 g/6 oz skinned sole fillets or red mullet
   fillets, small fresh anchovies, sprats or
   sardines
175 g/6 oz squid, cleaned
175 g/6 oz raw medium prawns, peeled
175 g/6 oz whitebait
175 g/6 oz cooked fresh mussels, shelled
oil, for deep-frying
salt
lemon halves, to serve
PASTELLA
450 ml/¾ pint cold water
150 g/5 oz plain white flour
pinch of salt

1 To make the pastella, pour the cold water into a shallow bowl. Sift the flour with a good pinch of salt over the surface of the water. Whisk well until smooth; the batter should have the consistency of thick cream. Set aside.

2 Slice the fish fillets into thick strips. Cut the squid bodies into thick rings and slice the tentacles. Dry all the seafood well on absorbent kitchen paper.

3 Heat the oil in a deep-fryer or large saucepan to 180°C/350°F or until a breadcrumb dropped into it sizzles instantly. Drop the squid into the batter and remove with a slotted spoon. Slip the squid into the hot oil and fry for 2–3 minutes until golden. Remove with a slotted spoon and place on kitchen paper to drain. Keep the squid warm in a low oven with the door ajar.

4 Drop the sole strips into the batter, shake off the excess and drop into the hot oil. Fry for 2–3 minutes then transfer to kitchen paper. Drop the prawns into the batter, shake off the excess and fry for 3–5 minutes. Drain on kitchen paper.

5 Drop the whitebait into the batter, fry for 3–4 minutes then drain on kitchen paper. Drop the mussels into the batter, fry for 1 minute and, again, drain on kitchen paper.

6 Toss all the cooked seafood together and sprinkle with salt. Pile on to a warmed platter and serve immediately with the lemon halves.

Tuna Burgers

These spicy little patties of hand-minced fresh tuna, which are pan-fried or grilled on a barbecue, are delicious either hot or cold.

Serves: **6**

Preparation time: 25 minutes, plus standing and chilling

Cooking time: 12 minutes

500 g/1 lb fresh tuna, boned and skinned
50 g/2 oz stale breadcrumbs
about 125 ml/4 fl oz milk
2 tablespoons currants
2 tablespoons pine nuts
2 tablespoons chopped parsley
2 tablespoons freshly grated Pecorino or
   Parmesan cheese
1 egg, beaten
flour, for coating
salt and pepper
olive oil, for frying
Basic Tomato Sauce (see page 84), to serve
TO GARNISH
lemon wedges
basil leaves

1 Finely dice the tuna by hand – do not use a food processor or blender.

2 Moisten the breadcrumbs with the milk and set aside for 10 minutes. Squeeze out the excess moisture from the bread.

3 Put the fish into a bowl with the bread and mix in all the remaining ingredients. Shape into 12–18 small thick patties. Put the patties on a tray, cover and refrigerate for at least 1 hour for them to firm up.

4 Roll the patties in flour, shaking off any excess. Heat the olive oil in a large shallow pan and brown the patties on both sides, then turn down the heat and cook them gently for a further 10 minutes, turning over halfway through. Garnish with lemon wedges and basil leaves, and serve with tomato sauce.

Meat, Poultry and Game

Roast Pork Loin with Rosemary and Garlic

In the early morning markets in Tuscany, the aroma from the porchetta stalls – with their whole roast pigs, heavily scented with garlic and rosemary, which have been cooked all night in wood-fired ovens – is utterly irresistible. This is how to cook it at home. Ask your butcher to bone the loin, but to give you the bones, and to remove the skin and score it to make crackling.

Serves: **6**

Preparation time: 25 minutes

Cooking time: 1½ hours

Oven temperature: 240°C/475°F/Gas Mark 9

1.75 kg/3½ lb loin of pork, bones removed
6 large garlic cloves
4 tablespoons chopped rosemary
2 tablespoons olive oil
300 ml/½ pint dry white wine
4 rosemary sprigs
salt and pepper
crusty bread, to serve

1 Put the loin fat-side down and, using a sharp knife, make deep slits all over the meat especially in the thick part.

2 Put the garlic and chopped rosemary in a food processor with at least 1 teaspoon each of salt and pepper (more will give a truly authentic Tuscan flavour) and make a paste. Push this paste into all the slits in the loin and spread the rest over the surface of the meat. Roll up the loin and tie with fine string.

3 Weigh the meat and calculate the cooking time, allowing 25 minutes to every 500 g/1 lb. Brown the pork all over in a frying pan in the olive oil, then set it in a roasting tin and pour the wine over it. Tuck in the rosemary sprigs.

4 Place the bones in another roasting tin, convex-side up. Rub the pork skin with a little oil and salt and drape it over the bones. Place the tin of crackling on the top shelf of a preheated oven, 240°C/475°F/Gas Mark 9, and the pork on the bottom or middle shelf. Roast for 20 minutes then turn down the heat to 200°C/400°F/Gas Mark 6 and roast for the rest of the calculated cooking time, basting the pork every 20 minutes.

5 Serve the pork in thick slices with pieces of crunchy crackling and the pan juices, accompanied by crusty bread.

Beef Braised in Barolo

Barolo is a truly great full-bodied red wine from Piedmont, which is not ready to drink until it is at least 3–4 years old. Made from the Nebbiolo grape, it turns a deep red brown colour with age. Normally a whole piece of beef is marinated in hearty Barolo, then slowly braised and served sliced with the puréed sauce. In this version, the wine is reduced before cooking to concentrate the flavour and the meat is cut into large chunks. The sauce is dark and luxuriant after the long slow cooking. A very good dish for a crowd.

Serves: **6–8**

Preparation time: 35 minutes, plus marinating

Cooking time: 2–3 hours

Oven temperature: 160°C/325°F/Gas Mark 3

2 bottles Barolo or other good red wine
1.5 kg/3 lb stewing beef, such as shin, chuck or
  skirt, trimmed and cut into 7 cm/3 inch pieces
2 onions, roughly chopped
2 carrots, chopped
1 celery stick, chopped
2 bay leaves
2 large thyme sprigs
6 peppercorns
2 allspice berries, crushed
3 tablespoons olive oil
2 tablespoons tomato purée or sun-dried
  tomato purée
Beef Stock (see page 8)
salt and pepper
chopped parsley, to serve

1 Pour the wine into a large saucepan or sauté pan, bring to the boil and continue to boil hard until it has reduced by half. Leave to cool completely.

2 Place the meat in a large strong polythene bag with the onions, carrots, celery, bay leaves, thyme, peppercorns and crushed allspice berries. Pour in the cooled wine. Shake the bag to mix the ingredients together then seal it tightly and put it in the refrigerator to marinate overnight.

3 Pour the contents of the bag into a colander or sieve placed over a bowl. Separate the meat from the vegetables and pat it dry with kitchen paper. Reserve the wine.

4 Heat the oil in a large flameproof casserole and brown the meat well in batches. Return all the meat to the casserole and stir in the vegetables, herbs and spices.

5 Pour over the reserved wine and stir in the tomato purée. Add enough stock to cover the meat and vegetables. Bring to the boil, turn down the heat, cover the casserole and simmer gently for 2–3 hours or until the meat is very tender. Alternatively, cook in a preheated oven, 160°C/325°F/Gas Mark 3, for 2–3 hours. Top up with beef stock if the liquid evaporates too quickly.

6 Lift the meat out of the casserole with a slotted spoon and put it into a bowl. Remove the bay leaves from the sauce then pour the sauce into a liquidizer or food processor and blend until smooth. The sauce will look pale, but will darken when reheated. Taste and season. The sauce should be quite thick; if not, boil to reduce it.

7 Stir the meat into the sauce and reheat until it is piping hot. Serve sprinkled with chopped parsley.

Devilled Fillet Steaks

Italians love meat cooked very rare. These steaks are served with a rich, piquant sauce.

Serves: **4**

Preparation time: 10 minutes

Cooking time: 15 minutes

2 tablespoons olive oil
4 fillet steaks, about 175 g/6 oz each
2 tablespoons balsamic vinegar
75 ml/3 fl oz dry red wine
4 tablespoons Beef Stock (see page 8)
2 garlic cloves, chopped
1 teaspoon crushed fennel seeds
1 tablespoon sun-dried tomato purée
½ teaspoon crushed dried chillies
salt and pepper
TO GARNISH
chopped parsley
rocket (optional)

1 Heat the oil in a nonstick frying pan. When it is smoking hot, add the steaks and cook for about 2 minutes on each side, if you want your steaks to be medium rare.

2 Take the steaks out of the pan, season them with salt and pepper and keep them warm. Pour the vinegar, red wine and stock into the pan, boil for 30 seconds, scraping up any sediment from the bottom of the pan.

3 Add the garlic and fennel seeds and whisk in the sun-dried tomato purée and chillies, to taste. Bring the sauce to the boil and boil hard to reduce until syrupy.

4 Transfer the steaks to warm plates, pouring any juices from them into the sauce. Bring the sauce back to the boil, then taste and season with salt and pepper. Pour the sauce over the steaks and serve immediately garnished with chopped parsley and a rocket salad, if liked. Slice the steaks before serving, if you wish.

Veal Escalopes with Lemon

Serves: **4**

Preparation time: 10 minutes

Cooking time: 10 minutes

4 x 175 g/6 oz veal escalopes
flour, for dusting
1 tablespoon olive oil
50 g/2 oz butter
finely grated rind and juice of 1 lemon
150 ml/¼ pint dry white wine
2 tablespoons chopped parsley
salt and pepper
parsley sprigs, to garnish
lemon wedges, to serve

1 Trim the veal escalopes of any gristle around the edge. Place between sheets of clingfilm and flatten thinly with a meat mallet or rolling pin, being careful not to tear the flesh. Dip the escalopes in seasoned flour, shaking off any excess.

2 Heat the oil and butter together in a frying pan. When it is foaming add the escalopes, 2 at a time, and fry over a brisk heat for 2 minutes on each side, pressing them down with a fish slice to keep them flat. Remove the escalopes from the pan and keep warm.

3 Add the lemon rind and juice and wine to the pan, stirring and scraping to dislodge any sediment. Boil for 2 minutes. Taste and season with salt and pepper. Stir in the parsley and pour the sauce over the escalopes. Garnish with parsley sprigs and serve with lemon wedges.

VARIATION • You can use turkey instead of veal escalopes, if you prefer.

Veal and Sage Escalopes

Serves: **4**

Preparation time: 15 minutes

Cooking time: 10 minutes

8 x 125 g/4 oz veal or turkey escalopes
8 slices of prosciutto or Parma ham
8 sage leaves
flour, for dusting
125 g/4 oz butter
200 ml/7 fl oz dry Marsala
salt and pepper
sage leaves, to garnish

1 Trim the veal escalopes of any gristle around the edge. Place between sheets of clingfilm and flatten thinly with a meat mallet or rolling pin, being careful not to tear the flesh.

2 Season each escalope with a little salt. Lay a slice of ham on each one, put a sage leaf on top and secure them through the middle as if you were taking a large stitch with a cocktail stick. These escalopes are not rolled up. Dust each of the escalopes with seasoned flour on both sides.

3 Heat half of the butter in a frying pan and fry the escalopes, 4 at a time, for 2 minutes on each side until golden brown and tender. Remove from the pan and keep warm.

4 Add the Marsala to the pan and stir with a wooden spoon, scraping up any sediment from the bottom of the pan, and bring to the boil. Add the remaining butter and boil rapidly for 1 minute. Spoon the sauce over the escalopes and serve immediately, garnished with sage leaves.

VARIATION • Use sherry instead of Marsala, if preferred. You can also substitute turkey escalopes instead of veal.

Roast Leg of Lamb with Wine and Juniper

A Roman way with lamb, the anchovies melting away to give a delicious savoury flavour to the lamb and sauce.

Serves: **6**

Preparation time: 20 minutes

Cooking time: 1½ hours

Oven temperature: 160°C/325°F/Gas Mark 3

1.5 kg/3 lb leg of lamb
2 tablespoons olive oil
10 juniper berries, crushed
3 garlic cloves, crushed
50 g/2 oz salted anchovies, boned and rinsed
1 tablespoon chopped rosemary
2 tablespoons balsamic vinegar
2 rosemary sprigs
2 bay leaves
300 ml/½ pint dry white wine
4–6 thyme sprigs
salt and pepper

1 Trim the lamb of any excess fat. Heat the oil in a casserole in which the lamb will fit snugly. Add the lamb and brown all over. Remove and leave to cool.

2 Pound together 6 of the juniper berries, the garlic, anchovies and rosemary using the end of a rolling pin. Stir in the vinegar and mix to a paste.

3 Make small incisions all over the lamb with a small sharp knife. Spread the paste over the lamb, working it into the incisions. Season with salt and pepper.

4 Put the rosemary sprigs and bay leaves in the casserole and put the lamb on top. Pour in the wine and add the remaining crushed juniper berries and the thyme. Cover the casserole, bring to the boil then bake in a preheated oven, 160°C/325°F/Gas Mark 3, for 1 hour, turning the lamb over and replacing the lid every 20 minutes.

5 Raise the oven temperature to 200°C/400°F/Gas Mark 6 and remove the lid from the casserole. Roast for another 30 minutes. The lamb should be very tender and completely cooked through.

6 Carefully remove the lamb from the casserole to a warmed serving dish and keep warm. Skim the fat from the sauce. Add a little water if necessary and bring the sauce to the boil, scraping the bottom of the pan to mix in the sediment. Taste the sauce and season with salt and pepper. Pour into a sauceboat and serve with the lamb.

Italian Meatballs

Serves: **4**

Preparation time: 20 minutes

Cooking time: 1 hour 20 minutes

Oven temperature: 180°C/350°F/Gas Mark 4

2 slices of stale bread, crusts removed
75 ml/3 fl oz milk
4 tablespoons oil
6 spring onions or 1 small onion, chopped
1 garlic clove, chopped
750 g/1½ lb lean minced beef
2 tablespoons freshly grated Parmesan cheese
freshly grated nutmeg
300 ml/½ pint dry white wine
400 g/13 oz can chopped tomatoes
2 bay leaves
salt and pepper
basil leaves, to garnish
buttered noodles, to serve

1 Put the bread into a large bowl, moisten with the milk and leave to soak.

2 Heat half the oil and fry the onions and garlic for 5 minutes until soft and just beginning to brown.

3 Combine the meat with the moistened bread. Add the cooked onion and garlic, the Parmesan, nutmeg and salt and pepper to taste. Work together with your hands until the mixture is well mixed and smooth.

4 With clean wet hands, roll the mixture into 28 even-sized balls. Heat the remaining oil in a large nonstick frying pan and brown the meatballs in batches, then transfer them to a shallow ovenproof dish.

5 Pour the wine and tomatoes into the frying pan and bring to the boil, scraping up any sediment from the bottom of the pan. Add the bay leaves, season with salt and pepper and boil rapidly for 5 minutes.

6 Pour the sauce over the meatballs, cover with foil and bake in a preheated oven, 180°C/350°F/Gas Mark 4, for 1 hour or until tender. Serve with buttered noodles, garnished with basil leaves.

VARIATION • Use minced veal or pork instead of beef, if you prefer.

Regional Cooking

If you thought that the cooking was much the same all over Italy, you would be quite wrong. Italian cooking is intensely regional and varies substantially from one area to another, depending mainly on the local produce. A quick tour of the country will soon highlight these regional variations.

Piemonte and Valle d'Aosta

This is one of the best-known centres of gastronomy in Italy. The north has many culinary traditions linked with France, such as the love of cakes, pastries and desserts which are often enriched with chestnuts, cream and chocolate. This is an area renowned for its cattle and pig rearing and for the production of milk, cheeses and butter. Sausages and salamis of goose and pork are much prized, and butter is used more often than olive oil. Cooking is hearty, with many rich meat and game stews.

Lombardy

Historically, extreme wealth existed in this region side by side with extreme poverty. Traces of the two opposing cuisines can still be seen today, as in the rich meat stews and the poor man's polenta. This is fertile land, producing wheat, maize and rice, along with the breeding of cattle, pigs and sheep. A unifying factor is the generous use of butter and cream, with many famous local cheeses such as Taleggio, Gorgonzola and Mascarpone.

Liguria

Liguria was briefly part of France, and many similar local dishes can be seen in neighbouring Provence – the classic one being pesto, the wonderful green basil pasta sauce with olive oil, garlic, Pecorino cheese and pine nuts. This is the land of olive oil, herbs, fish and vegetables. Pasta is popular, with linguine and trenette being strong favourites.

Trentino–Alto Adige

This is mountainous land, with forests for rearing pigs and picking wild mushrooms, and plains for growing all types of grain for bread, including wheat, buckwheat and rye. Dumplings are popular in soups and stews, gnocchi and polenta are staple dishes, cream and cheese play an important part in cakes and desserts and trout abounds in the mountain rivers.

Veneto

An important trading city, Venice has adopted many culinary styles and ingredients from all who came here, especially the Arabs. Much of the cooking revolves around fish and seafood, although pork, poultry, wild duck and game also play their part. Also popular are rice and risotto, beans and bean soups and vegetables – the most famous being radicchio di Treviso.

Friuli–Venezia Giulia

The soft cured ham from San Daniele is produced in the hills, while polenta is a staunch favourite, eaten with grilled game. All the usual northern staples exist here, including potato gnocchi, bean soup, meat and game stews, risotto and cakes and pastries in the style of neighbouring Austria, with fruit being flavoured with spices and honey.

Emilia Romagna

This is a gastronome's paradise, with a rich and complex style of cooking ruled by the three great Ps – pasta, prosciutto and Parmesan. Tomatoes abound, along with sausages such as the famous mortadella. Balsamic vinegar comes from Modena, and fish soups dominate.

Tuscany

Tuscan cuisine is simple and rustic. Meats are grilled on an open wood fire, and the flavours are enhanced by cooking with wine, sage, rosemary and basil. Wild boar, hare and pheasant are much prized, along with wild mushrooms. Olives are one of the main local crops and Tuscan olive oils are among the best that Italy offers. Pecorino, beans and bread all play an important part in this robust cuisine.

Umbria

This land-locked area next to Tuscany has a similarly simple cuisine. Cooking takes note of the seasons, particularly in the autumn with the arrival of wild mushrooms and game. Pork products abound, with sausages, salamis and hams. The grill is the preferred way of cooking.

The Marches

Situated on the Adriatic coast, this is a quiet and rural area, rich in every type of truffle and wild mushroom. Pigs are kept not only to sniff them out but also because their meat makes wonderful salamis and hams. Pecorino is made from sheep's milk, polenta is eaten with meat sauce and vegetables such as tomatoes, artichokes and broad beans grow happily alongside fennel and large green olives. Fish soups are popular.

Abruzzi and Molise

Another quiet rural region of mountains and valleys, this area has a fondness for lamb, hams and salamis, game, cheese and mushrooms. Some of the best lentils in Italy are grown here.

Lazio

The cooking is plain, using olive oil, wine, garlic and rosemary. Pasta plays a great part, and baby lamb is spit-roasted or simmered with wine and juniper. Fish is plentiful but, considered historically to be a rich man's food, it has no tradition in Roman cooking. Artichokes and broad beans are great favourites.

Campania

Centred on Naples, this area is the beginning of the poorer south and the start of true Mediterranean cuisine. Oil is king and dried pasta is eaten twice a day. This is the home of the pizza, and little meat is eaten other than lamb, which is prepared for festivals. Pastries are stuffed with sweetened ricotta, almonds, candied fruit, raisins and pine nuts and flavoured with orange flower water.

Apulia and Basilicata

Apulia is the heel of Italy, home of ancient olive groves, where bread and dried pasta are the staples and the cooking is simple. Tomatoes are sun-dried and vegetables are preserved in olive oil. Fish and seafood are simply prepared and served with a squeeze of lemon, while hams and salamis are intense here in the south, and cheeses such as mozzarella are made daily to avoid the heat. Neighbouring Basilicata is a poor relative, which thrives on pasta and dishes flavoured with chillies.

Calabria and Sicily

Calabria is the toe of Italy and reflects an Arab influence in its cooking. Fish is cooked with raisins and pine nuts, and desserts are flavoured with honey, almonds and orange blossom. Tomatoes and aubergines feature in everything, topped with ricotta. Olives and olive oil abound, as do all citrus fruits. Fish is plentiful in the markets, with sardines, prawns, sea urchins, red mullet, sea bass, swordfish and tuna being favourites.

Sardinia

The Sardinians produce durum wheat and fruit, and prefer meat – cooked on open fires – to fish. Myrtle leaves are a popular flavouring, and mushrooms, wild fennel and asparagus grow everywhere. Cheeses, such as Pecorino, are a speciality of the region.

Sausage Ragù

Serves: **4**

Preparation time: 15 minutes

Cooking time: 1 hour 10 minutes

500 g/1 lb fresh Italian sausages
2 tablespoons olive oil
1 onion, finely chopped
2 garlic cloves, finely chopped
450 ml/¾ pint passata (strained
    crushed tomatoes)
150 ml/¼ pint dry red wine
6 sun-dried tomatoes, chopped
2 teaspoons fennel seeds
1 tablespoon chopped rosemary
2 tablespoons chopped sage
1 teaspoon freshly cracked black pepper
salt
rosemary sprigs, to garnish

1 Squeeze the sausages out of their skins into a bowl and break up the meat.

2 Heat the oil in a saucepan and add the onion and garlic. Cook for 5 minutes until soft and golden. Stir in the sausagemeat, browning it all over and breaking up the lumps with a wooden spoon.

3 Pour in the passata and wine and add all the remaining ingredients. Stir well and bring to the boil. Turn down the heat, half cover the pan and simmer very gently for at least 1 hour or until the oil separates on the top of the sauce and it is well reduced. Season generously with salt and pepper, garnish with rosemary sprigs and serve with soft or grilled polenta, pasta or gnocchi.

FOOD FACT • Fennel seeds are much used in Italian cookery and have a slight aniseed flavour. Italian sausages have a robust, spicy flavour and firm texture. They are available from large supermarkets and Italian delicatessens.

Lemon Chilli Chicken

This recipe was inspired by the tastes and flavours of outdoor cooking in the sunny south.

Serves: **4**

Preparation time: 25 minutes, plus marinating

Cooking time: 45 minutes

Oven temperature: 200°C/400°F/Gas Mark 6

1.75 kg/3½ lb free-range chicken
4 really ripe juicy lemons
8 garlic cloves
1 small red chilli, deseeded and chopped
2 tablespoons orange flower honey
4 tablespoons chopped parsley
salt and pepper
parsley sprigs, to garnish

1 Using a sharp knife and kitchen scissors, cut the chicken into 8 joints and put them into a shallow ovenproof dish.

2 Squeeze the juice from the lemons into a small bowl. Reserve the lemon skins.

3 Crush 2 of the garlic cloves and add them to the lemon juice with the chilli and honey. Stir well, then pour this marinade over the chicken and tuck the lemon halves around it. Cover and leave to marinate for at least 2 hours or overnight, turning once or twice.

4 Turn the chicken pieces skin-side up, scatter over the remaining whole garlic cloves and place the lemon halves cut-side down on top. Roast the chicken in a preheated oven, 200°C/400°F/Gas Mark 6, for 45 minutes or until it is golden brown and tender, or cook it on a barbecue, turning frequently and basting with the lemon marinade. Stir in the parsley, taste and season with salt and pepper. Serve decorated with the roasted lemon halves, garnished with parsley sprigs.

Chicken Cooked Under a Brick

This may sound a bizarre way to cook a whole chicken, but the flesh remains firm and juicy and has a slight barbecued flavour. The meat cooks quickly because it is the same thickness all over. Use the best quality chicken you can find.

Serves: **6**

Preparation time: 10 minutes

Cooking time: 25–30 minutes

2 kg/4 lb roasting chicken, preferably free-range
4 tablespoons olive oil
salt and pepper
TO GARNISH
chopped parsley
lemon wedges

1 Using kitchen scissors, cut along both sides of the backbone of the chicken and remove it. Place the chicken skin-side down, open it out and press down hard on the breastbone to flatten it. Turn the bird skin-side up. Make a slit through the skin on each side between the breast and the thigh. Fold the legs in and push the drumstick bone through each slit. The bird should be completely flat.

2 Heat the oil in a large heavy frying pan and place the chicken skin-side down in the pan. Put a flat lid or board on top of the chicken and a 5 kg/10 lb weight on top (bricks or stones will do). Cook for 12 minutes over a low to moderate heat until golden.

3 Remove the lid and weights, turn the chicken over, season well and replace the lid and weights. Cook for another 12–15 minutes or until the chicken is tender and the juices run clear. Leave to rest in a warm place for 15–20 minutes before carving. Garnish with chopped parsley and lemon wedges.

Hunter's Rabbit

This is a simple way to give rabbit the taste of the wild hills of Tuscany. The secret is in the reduction of the wine and the long slow cooking. In Tuscany, the rabbits are huge and are sold with the heads and livers, which are what really make the sauce special.

Serves: **4–6**

Preparation time: 20 minutes, plus marinating

Cooking time: 1–1¼ hours

1 large rabbit, liver reserved, jointed into
  8–12 pieces
4 large garlic cloves, finely chopped
1 tablespoon finely chopped rosemary
1 teaspoon salt
1 teaspoon cracked black pepper
1 bottle dry red wine
2 rosemary sprigs
3 tablespoons olive oil
2 tablespoons balsamic vinegar
2 tablespoons sun-dried tomato purée or
  tomato purée
a little Chicken Stock (see page 8) or water
polenta or Roast Potatoes with Garlic and
  Lemon (see page 194), to serve

1 Wash and dry the rabbit joints. Mix together the garlic, rosemary, salt and pepper and rub well into the rabbit pieces, especially on the cut sides. Cover and leave to marinate for at least 2 hours.

2 Meanwhile, pour the wine into a non-corrosive pan, add the rosemary sprigs and boil hard until the wine has reduced by half. Strain and cool.

3 Heat the oil in a large frying pan and fry the rabbit joints until well browned all over. Remove to a casserole. Fry the liver in the pan and add to the rabbit.

4 Deglaze the pan with the balsamic vinegar, then add the wine, scraping up the sediment from the base of the pan. Whisk in the tomato purée, season with salt and pepper then bring the sauce to the boil and pour over the rabbit. Add a little water or stock if it isn't completely covered. Return the sauce to the boil and simmer very gently for 45 minutes–1 hour.

5 To serve, lift the rabbit on to a warmed serving dish. Mash the liver into the sauce and reduce it to a syrupy consistency, if necessary. Pour the sauce over the rabbit and serve with polenta or roast potatoes.

Vegetables

Garlic Cloves Stewed in Olive Oil

These are a wonderful standby to add to all sorts of salads, potato dishes, purées, risotto and pizzas. The garlic cloves can be stored in the oil in the refrigerator for up to 3 months in a screw-top jar. The flavoured oil can also be used.

Preparation time: 5 minutes

Cooking time: 20 minutes

12 large garlic cloves
rosemary sprigs
thyme sprigs
300 ml/½ pint olive oil

1 Peel the garlic cloves and place in a small saucepan with the herbs. Cover with the oil and stew over a low heat for 20 minutes until the garlic is pale golden and soft. Leave the garlic to cool in the oil and use as required.

Roast Potatoes with Garlic and Lemon

These potatoes are browned in oil, scented with lemon and garlic, then steamed in their own moisture, and crisped again. You must use waxy potatoes or they will fall apart during cooking.

Serves: **4**

Preparation time: 10 minutes, plus soaking

Cooking time: 25 minutes

500 g/1 lb waxy potatoes, such as Desirée
4 tablespoons olive oil
4 garlic cloves, unpeeled
a few thyme and rosemary sprigs
finely grated rind of 1 lemon
25 g/1 oz butter
coarse sea salt

1 Cut the potatoes into quarters lengthways, cover them with cold water and leave to soak for 10 minutes. Drain, then pat dry.

2 Heat the oil in a flameproof casserole and, when it is really hot, add the potatoes and garlic. Reduce the heat and brown the potatoes all over. Stir in most of the herb sprigs and the lemon rind, cover the casserole and cook the potatoes in their own steam for 15 minutes.

3 Remove the lid and turn the heat up to evaporate any water and crisp the potatoes. Stir in the butter.

4 Tip the potatoes into a warmed serving dish and scatter with plenty of salt and more herb sprigs.

Parmesan, Olive Oil and Pine Nut Mashed Potatoes

This is quite simply the best mashed potato.

Serves: **6–8**

Preparation time: 10 minutes

Cooking time: 20–25 minutes

1.5 kg/3 lb potatoes, such as Desirée, peeled
150 ml/¼ pint fruity olive oil, plus extra to serve
125 g/4 oz freshly grated Parmesan cheese
salt and pepper
50 g/2 oz pine nuts, toasted, to serve

1 Boil the potatoes in salted water for 15–20 minutes until very tender. Drain and leave to steam in the colander for 5 minutes.

2 Push the potatoes through a potato ricer or mash them by hand. With an electric whisk, beat in the olive oil, then the Parmesan. Continue beating for a few minutes over the heat – the mash will be nice and fluffy. Season well with salt and lots of black pepper. Turn into a warmed serving dish, drizzle with more oil and scatter the pine nuts over the top.

Tomato and Aubergine Parmigiana

A variation on a theme – plum tomato wedges are used here instead of tomato sauce. This dish is almost a meal in itself.

Serves: **4**

Preparation time: 15 minutes, plus draining

Cooking time: 25 minutes

Oven temperature: 190°C/375°F/Gas Mark 5

1 large aubergine
olive oil, for frying
500 g/1 lb ripe red plum tomatoes, cut into
  wedges
50 g/2 oz freshly grated Parmesan cheese
salt and pepper
parsley, to garnish

1 Cut the aubergine into 2.5 mm/⅛ inch slices. Sprinkle with salt and place in a colander to drain for 30 minutes. Rinse well and pat dry with kitchen paper.

2 Heat the oil in a frying pan and fry the aubergine in batches until golden brown. Drain on kitchen paper.

3 Arrange the tomato wedges and the fried aubergine slices in alternate layers in a shallow ovenproof dish, with a sprinkling of Parmesan cheese between each layer. Season with salt and pepper.

4 Bake in a preheated oven, 190°C/375°F/Gas Mark 5, for 15–20 minutes until browned and bubbling. To serve, either cool the dish slightly and serve warm, or leave it to cool completely and serve at room temperature. Garnish with parsley.

Sweet and Sour Courgettes and Carrots

A much-loved combination of sweet and sour with the addition of sharp capers, this recipe is found in the south of Italy, particularly Sicily.

Serves: **4–6**

Preparation time: 10 minutes, plus standing

Cooking time: 10 minutes

4 tablespoons olive oil
375 g/12 oz courgettes, thinly sliced
375 g/12 oz carrots, thinly sliced
2 tablespoons white wine vinegar
2 tablespoons shredded mint
1 tablespoon salted capers, rinsed and roughly chopped
salt and pepper
mint sprigs, to garnish

1 Heat the oil in a frying pan and sauté the courgettes and carrots in batches until golden brown. As they are ready, remove them to a warmed serving dish with a slotted spoon, leaving any oil in the bottom of the pan. Season with salt and pepper.

2 Add the vinegar and mint to the pan and bring to the boil, then immediately pour this dressing over the vegetables and carefully toss to mix. Leave the dish to stand at room temperature for at least 30 minutes to allow the flavours to develop. To serve, scatter with the capers and garnish with mint sprigs.

Braised Baby Artichokes and Fresh Peas with Mint

Serves: **6**

Preparation time: 15 minutes

Cooking time: 25 minutes

2 tablespoons olive oil
6 spring onions, chopped
1 garlic clove, crushed
12 fresh baby artichokes
lemon juice, for brushing
75 ml/3 fl oz water
1 kg/2 lb fresh peas, shelled
2 tablespoons chopped mixed mint and parsley
salt and pepper
mint sprigs, to garnish

1 Heat the oil in a casserole, add the spring onions and garlic and cook gently for 5 minutes until they begin to soften. Set aside.

2 Trim the artichoke stalks to about 1 cm/ ½ inch. Break off the tough outside leaves starting at the base, until you expose a central core of pale leaves. Slice off the tough green or purple tips. With a small sharp knife, pare the dark green skin from the base and down the stem. Cut the artichokes in half. Brush the cut parts with lemon juice to prevent them from browning.

3 Return the spring onions to the heat and add the artichokes and water. Cover the casserole tightly and simmer for 10 minutes or until they are almost tender. Gently stir in the peas, mint and parsley and a little extra water, if necessary. Replace the lid and cook for a further 10 minutes if using fresh peas, but only 5 minutes if frozen. Season to taste and serve garnished with mint sprigs.

VARIATION • If fresh peas aren't in season, use 300 g /10 oz of frozen petits pois instead, defrosted before use.

Caponata

A delicious sweet and sour aubergine salad, served as an antipasto or as a vegetable. As always with any Sicilian dish, serve at room temperature. There are endless variations of caponata, which is delicious with beef.

Serves: **6**

Preparation time: 20 minutes, plus draining and standing

Cooking time: about 50 minutes

4 aubergines, cut into bite-sized cubes
2 tablespoons olive oil, plus extra for
  deep-frying
1 onion, chopped
2 celery sticks, sliced
8 really ripe red tomatoes, roughly chopped
1 tablespoon salted capers, rinsed well
50 g/2 oz green olives, pitted
3 tablespoons red wine vinegar
1 tablespoon sugar
salt and pepper
TO GARNISH
toasted chopped almonds
chopped parsley

1 Place the aubergines in a colander, sprinkle with salt and leave to drain for 30 minutes.

2 Meanwhile, heat a little olive oil in a saucepan and add the onion and celery. Cook for 5 minutes until soft but not brown, then add the tomatoes and cook for 15 minutes until pulpy. Add the capers, olives, vinegar and sugar to the sauce, season with salt and pepper and cook for 15 minutes.

3 Rinse the aubergines and pat dry with kitchen paper. Heat the olive oil in a saucepan and deep-fry the aubergines in batches until deep golden brown. This may take some time. Drain well.

4 Stir the aubergines into the sauce. Taste and adjust the seasoning. Allow the caponata to stand for at least 30 minutes before serving for the flavours to develop. Serve warm or at room temperature in a bowl topped with the almonds and parsley.

VARIATION • Instead of using fresh chopped tomatoes, use 400 g/13 oz canned tomatoes in their place.

Peperonata

This is a silky mixture of tomatoes and peppers to serve as part of a selection of vegetable dishes, or as an accompaniment to grilled fish or a frittata.

Serves: **4**

Preparation time: 10 minutes

Cooking time: 1–1¼ hours

3 tablespoons olive oil
2 onions, sliced
3 garlic cloves, chopped
2 yellow peppers, cored, deseeded and cut into thick strips
2 red peppers, cored, deseeded and cut into thick strips
1 kg/2 lb fresh ripe tomatoes, skinned, deseeded and chopped, or 2 x 400 g/13 oz cans chopped tomatoes
salt and pepper

1 Heat the olive oil in a saucepan, add the onions and garlic and cook over a gentle heat for at least 20 minutes until golden and caramelized.

2 Add the yellow and red peppers to the onions, cover the pan and cook for 10 minutes to soften the peppers.

3 Stir the tomatoes into the pepper mixture and simmer uncovered for 30–45 minutes until soft, thick and reduced. Taste and season with salt and pepper. Serve warm or leave to cool and serve at room temperature.

Breads and Pizzas

Focaccia

Traditionally baked on the hearth, focaccia is just as easily baked in a conventional oven. A terracotta bakestone heated in the oven will give pizzas and focaccia extra lift and a crisp base. Although focaccia can be made with any basic pizza dough, the secret of a truly light focaccia lies in three risings, and dimpling the dough so that it traps the olive oil while it bakes. Focaccia can be thin and crisp, thick and soft, and round or square. This one is made in a tin – but it can be moulded on a baking sheet to any shape you wish.

Makes: **2 thick 25 cm/10 inch loaves**

Preparation time: 25 minutes, plus rising

Cooking time: 20–25 minutes

Oven temperature: 200°C/400°F/Gas Mark 6

25 g/1 oz fresh yeast, 1 tablespoon dried active baking yeast, or 1 sachet easy-blend yeast
pinch of sugar
450 ml/¾ pint warm water
750 g/1½ lb plain white flour, plus extra for dusting
125 ml/4 fl oz good olive oil
coarse sea salt

1 If you are using fresh yeast, cream it together with the sugar in a medium bowl then whisk in the warm water. Leave for 10 minutes until frothy. For other yeasts, refer to the packet instructions.

2 Sift the flour into a large bowl and make a well in the centre. Pour in the yeast mixture and 3 tablespoons of the olive oil. Mix with a round-bladed knife, then your hands, until the dough comes together.

3 Tip out the dough on to a floured surface. Wash and dry your hands and knead the dough for 10 minutes until it is smooth and elastic. It should be quite soft, but if it is too soft to handle, add more flour.

4 Place the dough in a clean oiled bowl, cover with a damp tea towel and leave to rise in a warm place until doubled in size – about 1½ hours.

5 Lightly oil two shallow 25 cm/10 inch pie or pizza plates. Knock down the dough and divide it in half. Working on a floured surface, shape each piece into a round then roll out into a 25 cm/10 inch circle. Place them on the pie or pizza plates. Cover with a damp tea towel and leave to rise for 30 minutes.

6 Remove the tea towel and make dimples all over the surface of the dough with your fingertips. The dimples can be quite deep. Cover the dough once more and leave to rise until doubled in size – about 2 hours.

7 Pour the remaining oil over the dough and sprinkle it generously with salt. Spray the loaves with water and bake in a preheated oven, 200°C/400°F/Gas Mark 6, for 20–25 minutes. Transfer the loaves to a wire rack to cool. Eat the focaccia the same day or freeze as soon as they have cooled.

Olive, Caper and Sun-dried Tomato Focaccia

Makes: **2 thin 25 cm/10 inch loaves**

Preparation time: 25 minutes, plus rising

Cooking time: 20–25 minutes

Oven temperature: 200°C/400°F/Gas Mark 6

25 g/1 oz fresh yeast, 1 tablespoon dried active
 baking yeast, or 1 sachet easy-blend yeast
pinch of sugar
450 ml/¾ pint warm water
750 g/1½ lb plain white flour, plus extra
 for dusting
125 ml/4 fl oz good olive oil
50 g/2 oz sun-dried tomatoes (the dried kind),
 soaked and sliced
2 tablespoons salted capers, rinsed
250 g/8 oz black or green olives, pitted
coarse sea salt

1 If you are using fresh yeast, cream it together with the sugar in a medium bowl then whisk in the warm water. Leave for 10 minutes until frothy. For other yeasts, refer to the packet instructions.

2 Sift the flour into a large bowl and make a well in the centre. Pour in the yeast mixture and 3 tablespoons of the olive oil. Mix with a round-bladed knife, then your hands, until the dough comes together.

3 Tip out the dough on to a floured surface. Wash and dry your hands and knead the dough for 10 minutes until it is smooth and elastic. It should be quite soft, but if too soft to handle, add more flour.

4 Place the dough in a clean oiled bowl, cover with a damp tea towel and leave to rise in a warm place until doubled in size – about 1½ hours.

5 Lightly oil two shallow 25 cm/10 inch pie or pizza plates. Knock down the dough and knead in the sun-dried tomatoes, capers and half of the olives. Divide the dough in half. Working on a floured surface, shape each piece into a round and roll out into a 25 cm/10 inch circle. Place them on the pie or pizza plates. Cover with a damp tea towel and leave to rise for 30 minutes.

6 Remove the tea towel and make dimples all over the surface of the dough with your fingertips. They can be quite deep. Cover the dough again and leave to rise until doubled in size – about 2 hours.

7 Pour over the remaining oil, scatter with the remaining olives and sprinkle generously with salt. Spray the focaccia with water and bake in a preheated oven, 200°C/400°F/Gas Mark 6, for 20–25 minutes. Transfer to a wire rack to cool. Eat the focaccia the same day or freeze as soon as they have cooled.

Sage, Red Onion and Raisin Focaccia

Makes: **two 25 cm/10 inch loaves**

Preparation time: 25 minutes, plus rising

Cooking time: 20–25 minutes

Oven temperature: 200°C/400°F/Gas Mark 6

25 g/1 oz fresh yeast, 1 tablespoon dried active
   baking yeast, or 1 sachet easy-blend yeast
pinch of sugar
450 ml/¾ pint warm water
750 g/1½ lb plain white flour, plus extra
   for dusting
125 ml/4 fl oz good olive oil
4 tablespoons vin santo
50 g/2 oz raisins
2 small red onions, thinly sliced
4 tablespoons chopped sage
handful of sage leaves
coarse sea salt

1 If you are using fresh yeast, cream it
together with the sugar in a medium bowl
then whisk in the warm water. Leave for
10 minutes until frothy. For other yeasts, refer
to the packet instructions.

2 Sift the flour into a large bowl and make a
well in the centre. Pour in the yeast mixture
and 3 tablespoons of the olive oil. Mix with a
round-bladed knife, then your hands, until the
dough comes together.

3 Tip out the dough on to a floured surface.
Wash and dry your hands and knead the
dough for 10 minutes until it is smooth and
elastic. The dough should be quite soft, but if it
is too soft to handle, add more flour.

4 Place the dough in a clean oiled bowl, cover
with a damp tea towel and leave to rise in a
warm place until doubled in size – about
1½ hours. Warm the vin santo and stir in the
raisins, then leave them to plump up.

5 Lightly oil two shallow 25 cm/10 inch pie or
pizza plates. Knock down the dough and knead
in the raisins, half of the sliced onions and the
chopped sage. Divide the dough in half.
Working on a floured surface, shape each
piece into a round and roll out into a 25 cm/
10 inch circle. Place them on the pie or pizza
plates. Cover with a damp tea towel and leave
to rise for 30 minutes.

6 Remove the tea towel and make dimples all
over the surface of the dough with your
fingertips. The dimples can be quite deep.
Cover the dough again and leave to rise until
doubled in size – about 2 hours.

7 Scatter the remaining sliced onion and the
sage leaves over the loaves. Pour over the
remaining oil and sprinkle generously with salt.
Spray with water and bake in a preheated
oven, 200°C/400°F/Gas Mark 6, for
20–25 minutes. Transfer to a wire rack to cool.
Eat the focaccia the same day or freeze them
as soon as they have cooled.

VARIATION • Use a medium sweet sherry
instead of vin santo, if preferred.

Oatmeal Focaccia

This focaccia is made with a mixture of medium oatmeal and plain flour for the bread, with flaked oats and salt scattered over the top. The result is a thin, crisp but still moist focaccia with a crunchy golden topping. Make sure all the ingredients are at warm room temperature before you start. These loaves are best eaten the day that they are made.

Makes: **2 thin rectangular loaves**

Preparation time: 25 minutes, plus rising

Cooking time: 25 minutes

Oven temperature: 200°C/400°F/Gas Mark 6

2½ teaspoons dried active baking yeast
1 teaspoon sugar or honey
about 350–450 ml/12–15 fl oz warm water
125 g/4 oz medium oatmeal, warmed
500 g/1 lb plain unbleached white flour, warmed
2 teaspoons English mustard powder
1 teaspoon freshly ground black pepper
2 teaspoons salt
2 tablespoons fruity olive oil, plus extra
  for drizzling
3–4 tablespoons flaked oats (porridge oats)
coarse sea salt

1 Whisk the yeast and sugar or honey into the warm water and stir in the warmed oatmeal. Cover and leave to stand for 10–15 minutes until frothy.

2 Sift the flour, mustard, pepper and salt into a warm bowl, pour in the yeast mixture and add the olive oil. Mix to a soft dough. Add a little extra warm water if the dough looks too dry – it should be very soft. Turn out the dough and knead it for at least 10 minutes or until elastic.

3 Place the dough in a lightly oiled bowl, cover with a clean damp tea towel and leave to rise in a warm place for about 1 hour or until doubled in size. Oil 2 Swiss roll tins.

4 Knock back the dough, turn it out and divide in half. Pull and roll each piece to fit an oiled Swiss roll tin. Place the dough in the tins and press it into the corners with your fingers. Prick all over with a fork and scatter the oatmeal flakes and salt over the top. Cover with oiled clingfilm or a clean damp tea towel and leave to rise for 30 minutes–1 hour.

5 Drizzle the loaves with olive oil and bake in a preheated oven, 200°C/400°F/Gas Mark 6, for 25 minutes until golden. Remove from the oven and drizzle with a little more olive oil. Leave to cool on a wire rack.

Schiacciata

This is the flat bread of Tuscany, the word schiacciata *literally meaning flattened. These loaves can be small or large and are usually savoury although* schiacciata con uva *is a bread baked with Sangiovese grapes (the Chianti grape) and sugar, and is only seen at harvest time.* Schiacciata *may be baked with a variety of toppings.*

Makes: **six 15 cm/6 inch breads**

Preparation time: 25 minutes, plus rising

Cooking time: 15 minutes

Oven temperature: 200°C/400°F/Gas Mark 6

25 g/1 oz fresh yeast, 1 tablespoon dried active baking yeast, or 1 sachet easy-blend yeast
pinch of sugar
250 ml/8 fl oz warm water
625 g/1¼ lb plain white flour, plus extra for dusting
50 g/2 oz lard or hard white vegetable fat
2 tablespoons olive oil, plus extra for brushing
coarse sea salt
½ aubergine, thinly sliced and fried
TO SERVE
rocket leaves
Parmesan shavings

1 In a medium bowl, cream the fresh yeast with the sugar and whisk in the warm water. Leave for 10 minutes until frothy. For other yeasts, refer to the packet instructions.

2 Sift the flour into a large bowl and rub in the lard or fat. Make a well in the centre and pour in the yeast mixture, olive oil and salt. Mix together with a round-bladed knife, then your hands, until the dough comes together.

3 Tip out the dough on to a floured surface. Wash and dry your hands and knead the dough for 10 minutes until it is smooth and elastic. The dough should be quite soft, but if it is too soft to handle, add more flour.

4 Place the dough in a clean oiled bowl, cover with a damp tea towel and leave to rise until doubled in size – about 1 hour.

5 Knock back the dough and divide into 6 pieces. Shape them into neat balls, flatten and roll into 15 cm/6 inch rounds. Brush them with oil and sprinkle with salt, then cover with a damp cloth and leave to rise for 1 more hour or until puffy.

6 Dimple the dough with your fingers and brush it again with oil. Top with the aubergine slices and slide on to a baking sheet. Bake in a preheated oven, 200°C/400°F/Gas Mark 6, for about 15 minutes until golden and crisp. Sprinkle with rocket and Parmesan shavings, to serve.

VARIATION • Instead of the aubergine slices, cover them sparingly with either thinly sliced courgettes or red onions sautéed with garlic, herbs and olive oil. Alternatively, bake without a topping and serve sprinkled with shredded basil leaves and a drizzle of olive oil.

Taralli

These are a type of salatini, *a hard, crisp salty biscuit that you are sometimes offered if you are travelling by Alitalia. Native to Apulia and Basilicata, they are cooked twice, which makes them a type of biscotti. Keep them in an airtight tin.*

Makes: **about 40**

Preparation time: 15 minutes

Cooking time: 25–30 minutes

Oven temperature: 190°C/375°F/Gas Mark 5

500 g/1 lb plain white flour, warmed
1 tablespoon fennel seeds or freshly crushed
  black peppercorns
15 g/½ oz fresh yeast, ½ tablespoon dried active
  baking yeast, or 1 sachet easy-blend yeast
175 ml/6 fl oz dry white wine, warmed
125 ml/4 fl oz extra virgin olive oil, warmed
coarse sea salt

1 Sift the flour into a bowl and stir in the fennel seeds or black pepper.

2 Crumble the fresh yeast or dried active yeast into the warm wine and whisk until dissolved then stir the yeast mixture into the flour with the oil. If you are using easy-blend yeast, stir it directly into the flour, then add the warm wine and oil. Season with salt.

3 Mix the dough with a round-bladed knife, then your hands, until it comes together then turn it out on to a lightly floured surface and knead until firm, smooth and elastic. If the dough feels too dry, add a little water to form a soft dough.

4 Pull off a piece of dough and roll it into a 5 mm/¼ inch rope. Cut this into 5 cm/2 inch lengths and bend the ends together to form a ring, overlapping them and pressing them together. Place on a lightly floured tea towel. Repeat until all the dough is used up.

5 Bring a large pan of salted water to the boil. Drop the taralli into the water and scoop out with a slotted spoon when they rise to the surface. Drain on a clean tea towel. Dip the taralli in a dish of sea salt and turn, to coat. Shake off the excess salt. Arrange the taralli on an oiled baking sheet and bake in a preheated oven, 190°C/375°F/Gas Mark 5, for 15–20 minutes until pale golden. Transfer to a wire rack to cool.

Grissini

Nothing like the ones in packets, these grissini are fun to make and great served with drinks.

Makes: **16–20**

Preparation time: 15 minutes

Cooking time: 5–8 minutes

Oven temperature: 200°C/400°F/Gas Mark 6

½ quantity Basic Pizza Dough (see page 10)
flour, for dusting
slices of prosciutto, cut into strips, to serve
FLAVOURINGS
coarse sea salt
sesame seeds
poppy seeds
cracked black pepper

1 Working on a well-floured surface, roll the dough out thinly to a rectangle. Cut it into 5 mm/¼ inch strips following the long side of the rectangle. Lightly roll these strips and taper the ends.

2 Brush the grissini lightly with water and sprinkle with the flavouring of your choice. Put them on a baking sheet and bake in a preheated oven, 200°C/400°F/Gas Mark 6, for 5–8 minutes until crisp and brown. Leave to cool completely.

3 To serve, twist strips of prosciutto around the grissini.

FOOD FACT • Prosciutto is a cured ham, one example of which is Parma ham from Parma. It is pink in colour and marbled with white fat. It is sliced wafer thin and, unless it is incorporated in a dish as here, it is often served with melon or figs as an antipasto.

Classic Italian Flavours in the Storecupboard

There are obviously certain ingredients that you need to have in order to create authentic Italian flavours, though not many of them are to be found in the storecupboard given that true Italian cooking is based on so many fresh ingredients. That said, though, there are certain things that are indispensable.

Olive oil

Olive oil is virtually synonymous with Italian cooking and the choice of different oils is limitless – some are peppery, some fruity, some grassy, and others have a hint of almond. Choose a first cold pressed extra virgin olive oil for dressing salads and drizzling over meat, and a lighter, less expensive oil for cooking and baking. Do not keep oil for a long time – if you don't use a lot, buy smaller bottles.

Olives

Olives are a much prized crop, picked late in the year when green, or left to ripen on the tree until black or purple, by which time they are usually plumper and juicier and have a slightly milder flavour. Olives vary so enormously in flavour, it is always best to taste before you buy, if you can. Olives may be sold canned, bottled, in plastic packets or loose by the scoop from the barrel – which is obviously best because it enables you to taste. Green olives are also sold stuffed with anchovies, almonds or pimentos.

Black and green olive pastes are rich and salty and can be used as toppings, bread and pasta flavourings or even whisked into a dressing.

Anchovies

Canned anchovies are useful for adding piquancy to sauces, dips, bean dishes and stews. Choose a good quality brand of fillets packed in olive oil or salt. Soak them in milk or water before use to remove excess salt.

Vinegars

A good Chianti red wine vinegar is useful on salads and in sauces and marinades. The best vinegar of all though is balsamic vinegar, which is a rich sweet vinegar made from fermented Trebbiano grapes from Modena in northern Italy, and aged in oak casks for at least four years and up to 40 or 50. The price reflects the quality, so buy the most expensive you can afford. Use it on delicate steamed fish dishes, on grilled meats and to enrich sauces and dressings. It is especially good on strawberries.

Pasta

Keep a variety of pastas in your storecupboard: say, a packet of spaghetti, a packet of tagliatelle, a packet of large shaped pasta, such as conchiglie, and a packet of short dried pasta such as tubettini for use in soups. Check the sell-by dates from time to time.

Rice

Carnaroli rice is the Rolls Royce of short-grained rice for making risottos, though arborio is also good and is more readily available.

Flour

Italian breads such as focaccia and pizza dough are made with ordinary plain flour, as strong flour makes the dough too elastic and gives the wrong texture. Pasta is traditionally made with Italian 00 flour, which is extra-fine flour made from tender Italian wheat. Polenta flour is coarsely ground maize from northern Italy and is used to make either soft polenta porridge or the sliced and grilled polenta, which is served with grilled and roasted meats or game. Unfortunately, polenta is time consuming to cook and needs a good 40 minutes continuous stirring, though 'quick-cook' or 'instant' polenta takes just 5–10 minutes, while lacking the intrinsic texture and flavour of real polenta.

Capers

Capers are the flower buds of the caper plant, which grows wild all over Italy. The buds are either salted or preserved in vinegar. They are important to Italian cooking and add a piquancy to salads and sauces. They come in brine or vinegar, and can be large (in which case they need to be chopped before use) or small in size.

Beans

Borlotti, haricot, black-eyed and cannellini beans (known in Italian as *fagioli*) – either fresh or dried – are staples throughout Italy, particularly in Tuscany, and are used in hearty soups and simple salads. Fresh beans are especially good and have a lovely creamy texture. Dried beans need to be soaked in water overnight and then rinsed and drained before cooking in boiling water. Lentils are also used (the best come from Umbria), as are fresh peas and fresh young broad beans, which are eaten raw in great piles in late spring with Pecorino. Canned versions are a poor substitute, but will do in an emergency.

Dried mushrooms

Dried mushrooms, in the form of dried porcini or ceps, are highly prized, quite expensive and available from Italian delicatessens. Before using, soak them in warm water for 20–30 minutes. Just a few slices of this special and very Italian dried mushroom adds a delicious musty flavour to a dish, which can enhance any sauce, stew or risotto. Dried mushrooms are particularly good mixed with fresh varieties.

Pine nuts

Also called pine kernels, these little nuts are gathered from pine cones. They add both texture and flavour to many savoury dishes, as well as to cakes and biscuits. They are an essential ingredient in pesto sauce.

Sun–dried tomatoes

These originated in southern Italy and Sicily, where they are used to boost the flavours of sauces, soups and stews. They are used sparingly in Italian cooking and are not widely used. Their use in this country stems from the Californian influence. Sun–dried tomato paste is also available.

Tomato purée

This adds richness to all sauces and stews and is therefore essential to Italian cooking. In addition, the pulp of ripe tomatoes – known as *polpa di pomodoro* – is also a useful ingredient to have in your storecupboard.

Truffles

The white Alba truffle is the most highly prized for its pungent flavour and aroma. The best come from Piemonte.

Spices

Of the many spices that have been used in the past 500 years, only a few of them are still in use today in everyday cooking. A good supply of pepper, cinnamon, cloves, nutmeg and saffron should serve you well.

classic italian flavours in the storecupboard

White Onion and Mozzarella Pizza

With no hint of tomato sauce, this is a succulent pizza where the onions are cooked to a creamy softness in olive oil before being spread on the pizza bases.

Makes: **two 30 cm/12 inch pizzas**

Preparation time: 30 minutes, plus rising

Cooking time: 35–40 minutes

Oven temperature: 240°C/475°F/Gas Mark 9

75 ml/3 fl oz olive oil
1 kg/2 lb onions, finely sliced
1 tablespoon chopped rosemary
2 teaspoons dried oregano
1 quantity Basic Pizza Dough (see page 10)
1 mozzarella, weighing about 150 g/5 oz, drained and thinly sliced
2 tablespoons freshly grated Parmesan cheese
12 anchovy fillets in oil, drained
15 black olives, pitted
salt and pepper
rosemary sprigs, to garnish

1 Heat the oil in a saucepan, add the onions and cook over a gentle heat for about 20 minutes, stirring occasionally, until they are completely soft and golden. They must not brown. Stir in the herbs and season with salt and pepper.

2 Knock back the pizza dough. Divide the dough in half and roll each one out, or stretch it with your fingers, to form a 25–30 cm/10–12 inch circle, about 5 mm/¼ inch thick. Slide the circles on to 2 well-floured flat baking sheets.

3 Cover the pizza bases with the sliced mozzarella then top with the onions. Sprinkle with the Parmesan and arrange the anchovy fillets and olives over the top.

4 Bake the pizzas in a preheated oven, 240°C/475°F/Gas Mark 9, for 15–20 minutes until golden and crisp. Scatter with rosemary sprigs and serve immediately.

Potato, Sausage, Feta and Onion Double-crust Pizza

This double-crusted filled pizza is sometimes known as a sfincione *throughout Sicily.*

Makes: **one 30 cm/12 inch double crust pizza**

Preparation time: 25 minutes, plus rising

Cooking time: 25–30 minutes

Oven temperature: 240°C/475°F/Gas Mark 9

2 tablespoons olive oil, plus extra for brushing
1 potato, finely diced
1 onion, finely sliced
1 teaspoon dried oregano
250 g/8 oz fresh Italian sausage, skinned
1 quantity Basic Pizza Dough (see page 10)
plain flour, for dusting
125 g/4 oz salted ricotta cheese, crumbled
2 tablespoons chopped sage
2 tablespoons freshly grated Parmesan cheese
salt and pepper
sage sprigs, to garnish

1 Heat the oil in a frying pan and add the potato and onion. Cook for 3–4 minutes until the onion starts to colour, then stir in the oregano. Transfer to a bowl. Fry the sausage briefly, breaking it up and turning it over.

2 Knock down the dough and divide it in half. Roll each piece into a thin 30 cm/12 inch circle. Slide one circle on to a well-floured baking sheet. Spoon the potato and onion mixture on to this circle, spreading it almost but not quite to the edge. Dot with the pieces of sausage and cover with the ricotta and sage. Season with salt and pepper.

3 Brush the edge of the circle with water and put the remaining circle on top. Pinch and roll the edges to seal. Brush the top with olive oil and sprinkle with the Parmesan. Make 2 or 3 holes in the top of the pizza.

4 Bake the pizza in a preheated oven, 240°C/475°F/Gas Mark 9, for about 20 minutes until golden and crisp. Leave to stand for about 10 minutes before serving, garnished with sage sprigs.

VARIATION • Although feta is not an Italian cheese, it makes a good alternative to the salted ricotta in this recipe.

Tomato, Artichoke, Prosciutto and Garlic Sfincione

This pizza is a little thicker and has far more topping than you would expect from a Neapolitan pizza, so it is very moist.

Makes: **1 thick 30 cm/12 inch pizza**

Preparation time: 35 minutes, plus rising

Cooking time: 20 minutes

Oven temperature: 240°C/475°F/Gas Mark 9

15 g/½ oz fresh yeast, ½ tablespoon dried active
   baking yeast, or 1 sachet easy-blend yeast
pinch of sugar
250 ml/8 fl oz warm water
375 g/12 oz plain white flour, plus extra
   for dusting
2 tablespoons olive oil, plus extra for drizzling
½ teaspoon salt
3 tablespoons sun-dried tomato purée
1 mozzarella, weighing about 150 g/5 oz,
   thinly sliced
4 ripe plum tomatoes, cut into long wedges
8 artichoke hearts in oil, drained and halved
4 large garlic cloves, sliced
6 slices of prosciutto
3 tablespoons freshly grated Parmesan cheese
fresh basil leaves, to garnish

1 If you are using fresh yeast, cream it together with the sugar in a medium bowl then whisk in the warm water. Leave for 10 minutes until frothy. For other yeasts, refer to the packet instructions.

2 Sift the flour into a large bowl and make a well in the centre. Pour in the yeast mixture, olive oil and salt. Mix with a round-bladed knife, then with your hands, until the dough comes together.

3 Tip out the dough on to a floured surface. Wash and dry your hands and knead the dough for 10 minutes until it is smooth and elastic. It should be quite soft, but if it is too soft to handle, add more flour.

4 Place the dough in a clean oiled bowl, cover with a damp tea towel and leave to rise until doubled in size – about 1 hour.

5 Knock back the dough and roll it out, or stretch it with your fingers, to a 30 cm/12 inch circle, making sure the dough is thicker at the edges than the middle, then slide it on to a large floured baking sheet. Alternatively, press the dough into a rectangular oiled baking tray.

6 Spread the sun-dried tomato purée over the base of the pizza then arrange half of the mozzarella over it. Scatter over the tomatoes, artichoke hearts and sliced garlic. Scrunch up the prosciutto and drape it over the pizza. Scatter over the remaining mozzarella. Drizzle with olive oil and sprinkle with Parmesan. Bake in a preheated oven, 240°C/475°F/Gas Mark 9, for 15–20 minutes until golden and sizzling. Serve the pizza immediately sprinkled with fresh basil leaves.

VARIATION • Use dried oregano instead of fresh basil leaves for the garnish.

Pizzette with Tomato Sauce

These are little circles of fried pizza dough topped with a little tomato sauce, some mozzarella and basil, and served piping hot at celebrations.

Makes: **10–12 pizzettes**

Preparation time: 25 minutes, plus rising

Cooking time: 8–12 minutes

½ quantity Basic Pizza Dough (see page 10)
plain flour, for dusting
oil, for frying
1 quantity Salsa Rossa (see page 118) or
  Basic Tomato Sauce (see page 84)
1 mozzarella, weighing about 150 g/5 oz,
  drained and cut into tiny sticks
basil leaves, to garnish

1 Roll out the dough very thinly on a well-floured surface. Use an upturned glass or round biscuit cutter to stamp out about twelve 5 cm/2 inch circles.

2 Heat the oil in a wok or deep-fryer until a crumb will sizzle instantly when dropped in. Fry the pizzette, a few at a time, for 2–3 minutes or until puffed and golden. Remove with a slotted spoon and drain on kitchen paper.

3 Top each pizzette with a little salsa rossa or tomato sauce, a stick of mozzarella and a basil leaf. Serve immediately.

Desserts, Cakes and Biscuits

Watermelon Sorbet with Chocolate Chips

This is a great favourite in Sicily – so cool and refreshing. It is made with a hint of cinnamon and, in some cases, the very exotic jasmine flower water. You won't need a whole watermelon for this recipe, so keep the rest to eat on its own or use in a fruit salad.

Serves: **4–6**

Preparation time: 20 minutes, plus chilling and freezing

Cooking time: 5 minutes

750 g/1½ lb skinned, cubed watermelon
300 g/10 oz caster sugar
1 cinnamon stick
8 tablespoons lemon juice
pink food colouring (optional)
1 egg white
125 g/4 oz chocolate chips
dessert biscuits, to serve

1 Remove the seeds from the melon with the tip of a knife. Liquidize the melon in a food processor then, with the machine still running, tip in the sugar and blend for 30 seconds.

2 Pour the melon mixture into a saucepan and add the cinnamon stick. Bring slowly to the boil, stirring all the time to dissolve the sugar, then turn down the heat and barely simmer for 1 minute. Remove from the heat, add the lemon juice then leave to cool, adding a few drops of pink food colouring, if using.

3 When the melon mixture is cold, remove the cinnamon stick and chill the mixture in the refrigerator for at least 1 hour or overnight – this makes freezing easier.

4 For the best results, freeze the mixture in an ice cream maker. When it is half-frozen, after 10 minutes, lightly whisk the egg white and add it with the machine still on. Stir in the chocolate chips then transfer to a freezer container. Cover with nonstick baking parchment.

5 Alternatively, pour the mixture into a shallow freezer tray and freeze until the sorbet is frozen around the edges. Mash the sorbet well with a fork, whisk the egg white until stiff then, using an electric hand whisk, drop spoonfuls of the sorbet into the egg white, whisking all the time until the mixture is thick and foamy. Return the sorbet to the freezer to firm up, then stir in the chocolate chips when it is almost frozen. Freeze until solid. Leave the sorbet to soften in the refrigerator for 20 minutes before serving with dessert biscuits.

Chocolate and Hazelnut Parfait

Popular throughout Italy, this is a semifreddo, a meringue-based ice cream that doesn't need to be stirred during freezing. It can be made in a mould and turned out or served in scoops.

Serves: **6**

Preparation time: 20 minutes, plus freezing

Cooking time: 5–10 minutes

Oven temperature: 160°C/325°F/Gas Mark 3

125 g/4 oz blanched hazelnuts
125 g/4 oz very dark chocolate, broken into pieces
600 ml/1 pint double cream
2 eggs, separated
175 g/6 oz icing sugar
dessert biscuits, to serve
TO DECORATE
chocolate curls
cocoa powder

1 Spread the hazelnuts on a baking sheet and toast in a preheated oven, 160°C/325°F/Gas Mark 3, for 5–10 minutes until golden. Leave them to cool completely then grind very finely.

2 Place the chocolate in a heatproof bowl over a pan of hot water and leave to melt. Whisk the cream until it holds its shape, then fold in the nuts. Whisk the egg yolks in a large bowl with 2 tablespoons of the sugar until they are pale and creamy. Whisk the egg whites in another bowl until they form soft peaks, then add the remaining sugar, spoonful by spoonful, whisking between each addition until the mixture is very thick.

3 Stir the chocolate into the egg yolk mixture. Fold in the cream, then the meringue mixture. Turn into an ice cream mould or a freezer container and freeze for 12 hours until firm.

4 To serve, remove the semifreddo from the freezer and transfer it to the refrigerator to soften for 10 minutes. Decorate with chocolate curls and dust with cocoa powder. Serve with dessert biscuits.

Chocolate Sorbet

An incredibly rich sorbet for all chocolate lovers.

Makes: **about 900 ml/1½ pints**

Preparation time: 15 minutes, plus chilling and freezing

Cooking time: 10 minutes

600 ml/1 pint water
150 g/5 oz soft dark brown sugar
200 g/7 oz granulated sugar
65 g/2½ oz unsweetened cocoa powder
25 g/1 oz very dark chocolate (70% cocoa
   solids), finely chopped
2½ teaspoons vanilla essence
1 teaspoon instant espresso coffee powder

1 Put the water, both the sugars and the cocoa powder in a saucepan and mix together. Bring slowly to the boil then simmer for 4–5 minutes, whisking until the sugar dissolves. Reduce the heat and simmer for 3 minutes more.

2 Remove the pan from the heat and stir in the chocolate, vanilla and espresso powder until thoroughly dissolved. Pour into a bowl and cool over ice or leave to cool and chill in the refrigerator. Freeze in an ice cream maker according to the manufacturer's instructions. Serve immediately or transfer to a chilled container, cover and store in the freezer for up to 1 month. If you are using the sorbet straight from the freezer, transfer it to the refrigerator to soften at least 20 minutes before serving.

Caramelized Panna Cotta with Vanilla Apricots

Serves: **4**

Preparation time: 30 minutes, plus cooling and chilling

Cooking time: 25–30 minutes

600 ml/1 pint double cream
125 g/4 oz caster sugar
1 vanilla pod, split open
75 ml/3 fl oz granulated sugar
2 tablespoons water
4 tablespoons milk
1 tablespoon powdered gelatine or
  7 g/¼ oz leaf gelatine
VANILLA APRICOTS
8 ripe apricots
150 ml/¼ pint water
75 g/3 oz caster sugar
1 vanilla pod, split open

1 Put the cream, caster sugar and vanilla pod into a saucepan and heat until almost but not quite boiling, stirring occasionally. Remove the pan from the heat and leave to infuse for 20 minutes.

2 Melt the granulated sugar in the water in a heavy-based saucepan until it has dissolved then boil until the syrup turns to a golden caramel. Quickly pour the caramel into 4 x 150 ml/¼ pint ramekins or small moulds. Set them on a tray and leave to harden.

3 Pour the milk into a small saucepan and sprinkle on the gelatine. Heat the milk and gelatine gently over a low heat until the gelatine dissolves.

4 Stir the dissolved gelatine into the cream mixture. Bring to the boil, then immediately remove from the heat and strain into a jug. Pour the hot cream into the ramekins with the caramel. Leave to cool then chill in the refrigerator for several hours or until set.

5 Halve the apricots, remove the stones and cut each half into 3 pieces. Put them in a small saucepan with the water, sugar and vanilla pod. Bring slowly to the boil, then reduce the heat, cover and simmer gently for 5–8 minutes until the apricots are just tender. Leave to cool, then remove the vanilla pod and chill the apricots in the refrigerator.

6 Carefully loosen the panna cottas and turn them out on to individual plates. Serve with the vanilla apricots.

FOOD FACT • Although they are expensive, vanilla pods are full of flavour and can be reused several times. Wash the pods gently after use, allow to dry thoroughly, then store in an airtight container until needed again.

Vanilla Pears in Vin Santo

This recipe may seem extravagant, but the wine is perfect with the pears. Try using baby Italian pears, which are often available in the autumn, and halve the cooking time.

Serves: **6**

Preparation time: 15 minutes, plus cooling

Cooking time: 35 minutes

600 ml/1 pint vin santo
1 vanilla pod, split open
6 firm but ripe dessert pears
2 teaspoons arrowroot
1 teaspoon vanilla essence
chopped toasted hazelnuts, to decorate

1 Heat the vin santo in a large saucepan with the vanilla pod. Peel the pears carefully, but leave their stalks intact.

2 Stand the pears in the saucepan – they should just fit – and spoon over a little wine to prevent them discolouring. Cover the pan tightly so that no liquid is lost and poach the pears gently for about 25 minutes, turning them in the liquid occasionally, until they are tender. Leave to cool in the liquid.

3 Remove the vanilla pod from the pan, scrape out the seeds and reserve them. Lift the pears from the wine and place them on a serving dish.

4 Add the reserved vanilla seeds to the liquid in the saucepan and boil until it has reduced to 300 ml/½ pint. Mix the arrowroot with a little cold water, then pour into the pan and whisk over the heat until the sauce has thickened. Stir in the vanilla essence. Leave the sauce to cool then pour it over the pears. Sprinkle the pears with the chopped toasted hazelnuts to decorate.

VARIATION • Use almonds instead of hazelnuts and sherry instead of vin santo.

Walnut Cake with Strawberry Balsamic Sauce

A light moist sponge, this is especially good when made with fresh walnuts. The balsamic vinegar brings out the flavour of the strawberries.

Serves: **6**

Preparation time: 20 minutes, plus chilling

Cooking time: 45 minutes–1 hour

Oven temperature: 180°C/350°F/Gas Mark 4

375 g/12 oz walnut pieces
4 eggs, separated
250 g/8 oz caster sugar
finely grated rind of 1 lemon
icing sugar, to decorate
STRAWBERRY BALSAMIC SAUCE
500 g/1 lb fresh strawberries
3 tablespoons water
2 tablespoons icing sugar
1 tablespoon balsamic vinegar

1 Grease, flour and base-line a 23 cm/9 inch spring-form tin.

2 Whizz the walnuts in a blender or food processor until they are finely ground but not greasy.

3 Put the egg yolks and sugar into a large bowl and whisk with an electric beater until they are pale and creamy. Fold in the ground walnuts and lemon rind. Whisk the egg whites in a separate bowl until stiff then carefully fold them into the nut mixture. Gently pour the sponge mixture into the prepared tin.

4 Bake the sponge in a preheated oven, 180°C/350°F/Gas Mark 4, for 45 minutes–1 hour until risen and firm. Leave the sponge to cool in the tin; it will shrink away from the edges. When the sponge is cold, remove it from the tin and dredge with icing sugar.

5 To make the strawberry sauce, hull and halve the strawberries and put them into a saucepan with the water and sugar. Heat slowly until the juices start to run then pour into a liquidizer or food processor and blend with the balsamic vinegar until smooth. Sieve the sauce to remove the seeds, if you like, then pour it into a bowl, cover and chill in the refrigerator until required.

6 Serve the cake in thin wedges with the strawberry sauce drizzled over the top.

Panettone

This is a classic Christmas recipe, a cross between a bread and a cake; it is light, buttery and rich, studded with fruit and candied peel. Serve at room temperature and eat it with a glass of dessert wine, or a cup of tea.

FOOD FACT • Panettone originates from Milan and because of the high butter content it keeps well. It takes time to rise, so start preparing it early in the day – don't be tempted to let it rise in too hot a place once the butter has been incorporated or the butter will melt and the dough will be greasy. Panettone is normally cut into horizontal slices, the top one being removed and replaced. It is kept closely wrapped so that it doesn't dry out. Store in the refrigerator where it will keep for up to 3 weeks. According to tradition, a piece is kept aside to eat on 3rd February, the feast day of St Biagio, the protector of throats.

Makes: **1 large panettone**

Preparation time: 25 minutes, plus rising

Cooking time: 55 minutes

Oven temperature: 200°C/400°F/Gas Mark 6

1 tablespoon active dried yeast
150 ml/¼ pint warm milk
about 500 g/1 lb strong plain white flour,
  plus extra for dusting
2 teaspoons salt
1 egg, plus 4 egg yolks
75 g/3 oz caster sugar
finely grated rind of 1 lemon
finely grated rind of 1 orange
175 g/6 oz unsalted butter, softened
125 g/4 oz raisins
50 g/2 oz chopped candied orange and
  lemon peel

1 Line a deep 16 cm/6½ inch cake tin with a double strip of nonstick baking parchment which projects 12.5 cm/5 inches above the rim. Also line the bottom of the tin with baking parchment.

2 Dissolve the yeast in 4 tablespoons of the warm milk in a large bowl. Cover the bowl with a tea towel and leave in a warm place for 10 minutes until frothy. Stir in 125 g/4 oz of the flour and the remaining warm milk. Cover and leave to rise for 30 minutes.

3 Sift the remaining flour and salt on to the yeast mixture. Beat together the egg and egg yolks. Make a well in the flour and add the beaten eggs, sugar and grated lemon and orange rind and mix to an elastic dough. Add a little more flour if necessary, but keep the dough quite soft.

4 Work in the softened butter. Cover and leave to rise for 2–4 hours until doubled in size. Meanwhile, chop the candied peel. Knock the dough down and knead in the fruit.

5 Place the dough in the tin, cut a cross on the top with a very sharp knife, cover and leave to rise to 2.5 cm/1 inch above the top of the tin. Bake in a preheated oven, 200°C/400°F/Gas Mark 6, for 15 minutes then lower the heat to 180°C/350°F/Gas Mark 4 and bake for about 40 minutes until well risen and golden. Leave to cool in the tin for 10 minutes then transfer to a wire rack to cool completely.

Variation:
Little Panettone

1 Line 6 clean condensed soup cans with a strip of nonstick baking parchment projecting 6.5 cm/2½ inches above the rims. Line the bottoms of the cans with baking parchment.

2 Make the dough as in the main recipe. Divide it into 6 even pieces and roll into fat sausages that will easily fit the lined tins. Place the dough in the tins. Cut a cross on the top of each one with a very sharp knife, then cover and leave to rise in a warm place for 1–2 hours until the dough rises 2.5 cm/1 inch above the top of the tins.

3 Bake in a preheated oven, 200°C/400°F/Gas Mark 6, for 15 minutes then lower the heat to 180°C/350°F/Gas Mark 4 and bake for about 20 minutes until well-risen and golden. Cool the little panettone as for the main recipe, but keep tins for repacking them as presents.

Pistachio and Pine Nut Biscotti

These light, crunchy biscuits studded with toasted pistachio nuts and with a hint of lemon are the ideal way to round off a perfect Italian meal.

Makes: **50**

Preparation time: 20 minutes

Cooking time: 50 minutes–1 hour

Oven temperature: 160°C/325°F/Gas Mark 3

175 g/6 oz shelled pistachio nuts
2 tablespoons pine nuts
125 g/4 oz unsalted butter, softened
200 g/7 oz granulated sugar
2 eggs, beaten
finely grated rind of 1 lemon
1 tablespoon Amaretto di Saronno
about 375 g/12 oz plain white flour
1½ teaspoons baking powder
½ teaspoon salt
75 g/3 oz coarse polenta

1 Spread the pistachios and pine nuts on a baking sheet and toast in a preheated oven, 160°C/325°F/Gas Mark 3, for 5–10 minutes until golden. Leave the nuts to cool but leave the oven on.

2 Cream the butter with the sugar in a large bowl until just mixed. Beat in the eggs, lemon rind and Amaretto. Sift together the flour, baking powder and salt in a separate bowl, then stir into the butter mixture with the polenta. Stir in the pistachios and pine nuts.

3 Turn the dough on to a floured work surface and knead until smooth. The dough should be soft but not sticky.

4 Divide the dough into quarters and roll each piece into a sausage 5 cm/2 inch long and 1.5 cm/¾ inch thick and flatten it slightly. Place the sausages on 2 greased baking sheets and bake in the oven for about 35 minutes until just golden around the edges.

5 Leave to cool slightly then cut diagonally into 1 cm/½ inch thick slices. Place the biscotti cut-side down on the baking sheets and bake for another 10–15 minutes until golden brown and crisp. Watch that these do not burn – they will taste bitter. Transfer the biscotti to a wire rack to cool completely.

FOOD FACT • Biscotti are traditionally served with a glass of vin santo, a sweet dessert wine from Tuscany. The way to eat them is to dip them in the wine and munch – they are very moreish! These biscotti can be stored in an airtight tin for up to 1 week.

Index

Acknowledgments

Special photography: Ian Wallace

Special photography home economist: Louise Pickford